To Brook
Thank
you have done for me.
It is such a dream come
true
I could not have done
it without your belief

BIG
DREAMS

That I could actually
get a published book.
Many Thanks for believing
in me.

Donna Barnes

BIG
DREAMS
Essays on Recreating a Life

Donna Brazzi Barnes

SHE WRITES PRESS

Published 2022
Printed in the United States of America
Print ISBN: 978-1-64742-186-1
E-ISBN: 978-1-64742-188-5

Library of Congress Control Number: 2022901401

For information, address:
She Writes Press
1569 Solano Ave #546
Berkeley, CA 94707

Interior design by Tabitha Lahr

She Writes Press is a division of SparkPoint Studio, LLC.

All company and/or product names may be trade names, logos, trademarks, and/or registered trademarks and are the property of their respective owners.

Names and identifying characteristics have been changed to protect the privacy of certain individuals.

Author's Note: The names and identities of certain characters have been changed to protect the privacy of friends, but this story is true as I experienced it.

Contents

"The personal essayist looks for the truths that connect us all in the details of her own history, her experience of gender or loss or travel. The further paradox is that the more idiosyncratic these experiences seem, and the more specific the details of their telling, the more clearly they seem to strike the universal chord."

—MARION WINIK

My coming out of a deep sleep inspired this collection of essays. There was no Prince Charming to wake me with a kiss. I learned the hard way to examine and challenge the culture that prescribed women's roles in marriage, motherhood, and work. The awakening began in the early 1960s, though challenging these roles was a long journey culminating in career changes in the 1990s. This book of essays includes the longing of a young girl from Napa, California, a young woman leaving home, a woman marrying at age twenty-seven, the challenge of being the wife of a minister, and the struggles of a new graduate starting a career. Mothering my daughter gave me the courage to stop questioning cultural assumptions for women and take action. Returning to graduate school for a doctorate in sociology gave me the language to speak. Female friendships, Goddess rituals, the women at the writers' community called Hedgebrook, female partners at clergy retreats, and my daughter encouraged me and continue to support the choices I made.

Dedication

I dedicate my book to my daughter, Monica Bill Barnes. She has been my emotional support from a very young age. She is the one who always has my back. We have been close since the day I gave birth to her. She came out of my womb with a tightly closed fist. I considered that a sign, "Power to Women."

I also want to acknowledge those writers who have read drafts of my work, especially Brooke Warner who has been my constant reader, offering feedback to make my writing stronger. I have been supported by women writers and friends from my writers' residencies, Hedgebrook, The Anderson Center, and Ragdale. Monica has believed in me and continually encouraged me to write. She has been invaluable in the editing process, as well as Kayla Hansen who also helped edit my manuscript. Monica believes and has faith in me even when I doubt myself. And there is no limit to the love she gives me.

I Will Send the

Police after You

I was sitting on the couch at a right angle to my mother, who sat nearby in her chair. It was June of 1958 in what was then the small town of Napa, California. Mom was knitting wool socks for Dad despite the oppressing summer heat.

Just a few days earlier, I had graduated from high school with honors and a scholarship. Mom, upon reading my letter of acceptance that came in the mail that day from the prestigious University of California at Berkeley, declared, "If you go, I will send the police after you."

I was hoping for a smooth transition from dependent daughter to independent university freshman. Looking back, I realize I was challenging cultural assumptions embedded in my mother's perception of women's place in the world. Her response, after the threat of the police, was, "The only reason women go to college is to get a husband."

Leaving my small town for a larger world was a dream that was shared by my best friends who were going away to college. This path was blocked by my mother's expectations of me. Like my two older sisters, she felt free tuition at the local junior college was good enough. She gave me the impression that I was aiming above my station as the third daughter in a working-class Swiss–Italian family. This wasn't easy for me. I took the only path available, living at home and postponing my entry into university and my plan to leave my small town for a larger world.

In junior college, I aspired to go to medical school. My male counselor said, "My dear, women who go to medical school don't marry or have children." At that low point, I was beginning to understand that assumptions about women filtered into other institutions beyond my family.

I resigned myself with regret to forge ahead and take what was "prescribed" for me. I went to school in the morning, worked in the afternoon, and studied late into the night. The president of the Napa Junior College Board of Trustees was a dentist. Because I was an honor student, he bestowed upon me the job of dental assistant. I found the offer insulting. However, the money I earned would help me pay for my future university education, so I took the job.

Like any heroine in her own novel, I secretly plotted my departure by accepting two years of purgatory: earning top grades in college courses, working as a dental assistant, saving money, and forsaking a social life to study late into the night while being impossible to live with. In other words, I was the bitch in the house.

My hard work paid off. In 1962 I graduated from UC San Francisco as a dental hygienist. This was not my preferred vocation, but I enjoyed my independence and the science courses. I especially enjoyed the clinical experience. I did not enjoy the simplistic dental hygiene courses taught by frustrated older unmarried women.

At age forty-six, I returned to UC San Francisco and earned a PhD in Sociology in 1992. I immediately secured my dream job as senior lecturer at California State University, Hayward, now called East Bay, teaching women's studies from 1992 to 2008. Some of the students shared experiences remarkably similarities to mine. For example, one student was told she should not study computer science because it was "a man's field." Even worse, she would be reducing her chance of marriage. Older female students found their families were not supportive of their returning to school and leaving a secretarial or dental hygienist job. One returning student sent her announcement that she was graduating from UC Berkeley. She added, "Dr. Barnes, you were the only person who believed in me."

Growing up Is Hard

Growing up is hard. And I didn't make it any easier for myself. Not that I rebelled in an overt, screaming-meanie way. I had watched my eldest sister do that with repeated failure. Her rebellion was about when she could get her driver's license or how late she could stay out on a date or other issues I was not privy to.

I took on a different issue, and a different tactic from my sister. My journey of resistance was to the culturally assumed woman's role. In my own determined and less confrontational manner, I rejected the cultural assumption of the woman's exclusive role as housewife in the pre-feminist era of the late forties into the early sixties. This battle had not been fought yet. My journey of challenging woman's place was uncharted, without the benefit of parental advice or the necessary skills that would have helped.

When I was growing up, my mother was the iconic example of the woman's culturally prescribed role. She had a high school education, as some education was acceptable, just not too much. She was nineteen when she married my dad, within the expected age range; much past age twenty-one she would have been labeled an "old maid." Mom and Dad had four children, three girls and one boy, within ten years. I was the third daughter, followed five years later by my brother.

My mom excelled at her job when a woman's full-time work was mothering and running the home, with all the chores that involved. She was always there when I arrived home from school and had a hot meal ready when Dad came home from work. She made all our clothes, dressing her three girls in matching coats, dresses, and pajamas, and knitting our sweaters, hats, and mittens. For my doll, she made matching pajamas, sweaters, and blankets. She also made socks and sweaters for Dad and later for my brother. Dad's socks always had a detailed design, such as a golf cart or a baseball and bat, on the side.

Mom crocheted tablecloths, knitted blankets and afghans, and designed and made beautiful dresses for herself. Her three knitted dresses were in rose, yellow, and green yarn, and she complemented them with matching pillbox hats with the same-colored veil. She helped maintain a garden, cooked everything from scratch, and had a stellar reputation for her cakes. At the Napa County Fair, Mom won prizes for her handiwork.

An added cultural weight and barrier to my challenging a woman's place was that my family was of Swiss–Italian heritage on both sides. The traditional roles of marriage, homemaker, and motherhood were seldom, if ever, questioned.

The one exception was my maternal grandmother, Nana. She had divorced her husband when my mom was young, maybe five or six years old. They moved to Napa from Lake County, just north of Napa, and Nana started her own laundry business. That evidently folded, but she continued to work at Green's or Sheldon's Dry Cleaners in Napa and Vallejo until she retired.

Nana might have been my ally in my journey. She lived with us until I was five or six. I have no knowledge of why Mom and Nana did not get along, or why she was asked or told to move out. I was sad when this happened, but too frightened to take Nana's side against my mother.

Even after Nana's death, I hesitated to confront Mom about what caused this separation, though I was thirty-two and eight months pregnant. Becoming a mother had the effect of bringing Mom and me to a more cordial relationship. It seemed too risky to disrupt our newly found common ground of motherhood in order to learn more of my family history.

Nana clearly took the road less traveled for women in the 1920s. As her granddaughter, I surely must have learned that some women could write their own destiny. However, divorce and disharmony with family was not my chosen path to liberation.

I was well into my adolescence when I took up my journey of resistance to the culturally assumed woman's role. Prior to that, I'd had my childhood dreams. My aspiration was to be a singer and have legs like Betty Grable, a film star of the forties and fifties who was known to have the most beautiful legs in Hollywood. When I was seven, she was my idol, but when I was tall enough to look in the dresser mirror and saw my short chubby legs, I abandoned that dream.

My childhood suspicion was that I was African American, and my parents and siblings would not tell me. As a child of five or six, I obviously did not know what this meant, because if I had, I could have looked in a mirror. Growing up in Napa, California, with a small, predominately white population of 22,000, I never saw a person of color. The first African American I encountered in person was in 1960 during my junior year of college when I was twenty. I initially thought he must be one of the most important people at UC San Francisco, because he was constantly being summoned over the public address system. It turned out he was the custodian.

This unfounded suspicion meant that, from a very early age, I knew I was different, even if my family did not recognize it, and that I would take a different path than that prescribed for a girl whose family had emigrated from an Italian canton in Switzerland. Similarly, I abandoned my aspiration of being a movie star like Betty Grable. Eventually, I came to realize my suspicion of being African American was not true. Disappointment can breed innovation and creativity. Thus I began an uncharted journey with passion and perseverance, without my parents' understanding, and therefore with their resistance rather than their guidance.

I remember as a child the pressure to conform in our family. We were discouraged from speaking Italian. We only heard it once week when my dad spoke it with his father, whom we visited every Sunday afternoon. I loved those visits when Dad and Grandpa sat on the porch drinking Grandpa's homemade wine, while my sisters and I played hide and seek in his front garden of tall beanstalks and various other vegetables. My mom stayed home with my baby brother.

But we were not allowed to learn Italian growing up. We were told firmly, "We are Americans. We speak English." Italy, under Mussolini, had allied itself with Hitler and Germany in World War II. There was prejudice against Italians for being on the wrong side of the war, and suspicions about the Mafia hung in the cultural air of my hometown. There were and still remain historical differences between Switzerland, which stayed neutral in war, and Italy's aggression of Mussolini's invasion of Libya prior to the buildup of WWII. It was important to our family that we were from the Italian part of Switzerland, and not from Italy. Mom would constantly remind us that we were not Italian but were *Swiss*–Italian.

The pronunciation of our surname had been Americanized from Brazzi (the Italian pronunciation would be "Bratzzi" with a role of the tongue on the "r") to Brazzi (with no role of the tongue on the "r" and an emphasized "a"). It served me well when I ran for commissioner of activities in high school and won on the slogan, "Let's be snazzy, vote for Brazzi."

I grew up knowing that, like my two elder sisters before me, I was expected to get two years of junior college education after high school, marry, and have children. It was assumed that my full-time job as an adult would be to make a home, support my husband in his work, and raise our children—just like my mom was doing. Mom would remind me to take useful courses in high school, like typing, business, and English, not the foreign language and science classes required for university admission. I can still hear her practical advice: "It's important to have a skill you can fall back on in case things don't work out," implying secretarial skills in the event of divorce or widowhood or another tragic event that might leave a dependent woman helpless. In high school, when I defied her and took college prep classes, she protested, "The only reason women go to college is to get a husband."

By the time I got to high school, the truth was I didn't know anything about preparing for or applying to college. The dean of women, who was also my best friend's mother, Mrs. Bowman, recognized my potential and guided me to enroll in college prep courses, against my mother's advice. Mrs. Bowman also mentored me through an application to UC Berkeley, her alma mater. I don't recall if I told my parents I was applying. If I did not, it was for concern that Mom would allege I was aiming too high.

Close to graduation, I received my letter of acceptance to the university. This was a moment of triumph followed by frustration. I had not thought through the cost of college, despite receiving a scholarship from the Business and Professional Women Foundation.

After much discussion, Mom's final words on the subject were, "If you go, I will send the police after you." I was not sure I believed her, but without my parents' financial support to augment my scholarship, I had to turn down the offer, live at home, and go to the local junior college.

During my two years of self-imposed, moody exile at home, I recalled one summer evening when I was eleven years old that inspired me not to give up hope. I had finished the last sentence of *Gone with the Wind*, alone in the bedroom I shared with my two sisters. It was evening as I marched through the narrow, darkened kitchen to the larger well-lit living room. I announced to my family, "If I do not mend my ways, I will be just like Scarlett O'Hara." Mom smiled dismissively, Dad nodded approval, and my siblings looked puzzled, except for my eldest sister who smirked. And then they all returned to their reading or knitting without any further comment. I knew right then that I needed a larger world to explore.

My dramatic announcement to my family was perhaps overstated. What were "my ways" as an eleven-year-old? Being obedient was one, following orders another, and questioning authority, but I was too fearful to act on my revelation.

Unlike Scarlett, I did know that my hometown was not big enough to have a life different from the one expected of me. But like Scarlett, I felt I could learn the skills I needed to pursue my dream. Unlike Scarlett, I did not want to end up divorced. I think the book propelled me to be vigilant and to not let the culturally accepted woman's role overpower my path of freedom of action.

I always knew Dad supported me. He had a very gentle way of parenting. I don't recall him ever lecturing me or being demanding. He seldom told me what to do. He did not so much give me advice but by his example of gentle kindness and geniality, he showed me how to live. And though he had only an eight-grade education, he did not stand in my way when I wanted to go to college. I knew if he'd had any knowledge about college, he would have shared it with me.

But what could have helped me was for Dad to challenge my mother's dominant opinion about women and college. Or to help me figure out why she was so opposed to my going away to school. He could have encouraged me to go to university, like my friends' parents did. It would have been very supportive to have a reasonable conversation about allowing me to borrow the necessary funds beyond my scholarship for housing and books needed for UC Berkeley. Instead, my mother threatened me with the police if I accepted.

My parents' lack of support and encouragement released my self-doubts. If I had not been endowed with Betty Grable legs, had I been endowed with the intelligence to succeed beyond my hometown high school and junior college? My dad always said, "When they passed out the brains, Donna was not behind the door." Meaning I was definitely a recipient. That gave me confidence as a child, but not as a woman coming of age.

During my two years of tuition-free junior college education, I worked and saved what I thought was enough money for my junior and senior years at UC San Francisco. But my money was only enough for one year, despite the fact that I was frugal and worked in the school cafeteria five days a week, making sandwiches before my eight o'clock class. When, in my senior year, the dean of the dental school told me I qualified for funding, I found out just how opposed my parents were to my accepting financial assistance. Instead, they loaned me enough money for my last year, which I paid back with interest two years after I graduated. I believe they were too proud to let another, even an educational institution, finance their daughter's education.

In adolescence, I had realized that my future would be in the larger world, beyond my hometown. I knew I would challenge my family's and the culture's assumptions about women. I did not know, however, that I would be hindered by these assumptions about women, marriage and work, and at times disadvantaged by them. I did not know I would be discouraged from applying to medical school because I was a woman. I did not know I would be paid less than a man for comparable work. I did not know I would be denied a credit card because I was a woman. In the 1960s, when I was entering UC San Francisco, a bank could refuse to issue a credit card to an unmarried woman, and if she were married, her husband was required to cosign. It took the Equal Credit Opportunity Act of 1974 to make these practices illegal. I did not know in 1963, when I made an appointment with a nationally known brokerage firm, that I would be dismissed with a smirk by a stockbroker of my own age and denied my request to open an investment account.

Experience is one thing. Knowledge and examination of one's life is another. Through marriage, work, and mother-hood, particularly mothering, I was compelled toward reflection and introspection. My journey led me through readings, spiri-tual retreats, writers' residencies, and conversations with women friends. In 1995 at Hedgebrook, a women writers' residency, I met Theresa. On the first night of my three-week residency, she greeted me with a big hug and a welcome as I walked into the farmhouse kitchen for dinner. As the evening went on with lively talk and jokes, some of which I didn't understand but laughed anyway—albeit too loudly and with poor timing—I felt intim-idated to hold my own in the conversation. I said something stupid that even now I'm embarrassed to admit. I'm not sure exactly what I said, but something asinine like, "One of my best friends is lesbian." Score zero out of ten on that one. What most added to my feelings of intimidation was that I hid enormous doubts about my abilities as a creative writer.

After dinner, Theresa invited me to go for a walk on the beach. She asked me how I was doing. I said, "What came out of my mouth was dumb, and I didn't get some of the jokes. I hope I didn't offend anyone." I was disappointed in myself and wondered what kind of an impression I had made. Theresa assured me that I was not the only one who felt intimidated.

I said, "I felt like I said some inappropriate things, especially about my best friend being lesbian. I felt I was not myself. I was more guarded. And the lesbian thing I am comfortable with, but I felt like I was perceived as square."

Theresa said, "It was obvious that you were uncomfortable. On my first night, I went to two of the writers to apologize for something I said."

As she walked me back to my cottage and hugged me goodnight, I felt better but with mixed feelings. I wrote in my journal that night, "I'm so intense, unsure, and elated."

As the weeks progressed, Theresa became a dear friend, and I came to treasure each of the other four writers.

Growing up I had an aspiration to be Betty Grable and a suspicion that I was African American. Neither turned out to be possible or true. Looking back with nostalgia peppered with experience, my family's and cultural expectations gave me the opportunity to become who I am the hard way. In truth, I wasn't given the skills I needed, but I learned them, often faking it until I could practice them. But isn't it the best way to own knowledge, by working hard for it rather than having it given to you?

I would have done some things differently, given the chance. I would have run for student body president rather than commissioner of activities, with my winning campaign slogan, "Let's be snazzy, vote for Brazzi."

I would have tried harder to find a way to reason with my mom and actively elicit help from my dad. In my own persistent way, I did confront her by breaking the stereotype of women of the fifties and sixties.

I would have believed my math teacher and the dean of student activities, Mr. Fatinos, who wrote in my yearbook, "Without a doubt one of the few outstanding students I've had the pleasure of working with. Keep your sights high, Donna. You can be anything you set your mind to. A job well done, in and out of the classroom."

I would have dismissed my male college counselor's advice when he said to me, "My dear, women who go to medical school don't marry and have children."

I would have set my sights higher and gone to medical school instead of settling for dental hygiene.

I would have asked the young stockbroker in 1963 to explain in detail why I could not open an investment account and hopefully watched him squirm as he ran out of excuses.

I would have learned earlier that money is a resource, not a limitation, and that, within reason, money does not have to dictate choices.

Though I didn't become a medical doctor, I am a doctor of philosophy. I've heard it said that PhD stands for "piled higher and deeper." And that suits me more than being a medical doctor. The mysteries of how people live their lives and how we are shaped by different cultural assumptions support and hinder us on our life journey. In the twenties and thirties, Mom was a stellar example of what was expected of a woman. And though my experiences in my family starkly confronted what I aspired for myself, she, along with Dad, did provide a physically safe place for me to grow up and taught me values of family loyalty, pride of heritage, and, by necessity, frugality.

I recognize that my family and culture were dominated by assumptions that were very hard to challenge, and that they hindered me. But with passion, determination, and perseverance, I shaped an identity that was different from my family's and cultural assumptions. And in the ongoing process, I shaped my life.

My experience continues to make me very grateful to women who took their fight public, women like Betty Friedan, Gloria Steinem, Billie Jean King, Anita Hill and many others who challenged female stereotypes and initiated the feminist movement.

This is where my passion lies. Passion does not always drive us to do the easy thing. What was not given to me I learned by observation and with unexpected help from people like Mrs. Bowman and Mr. Fatinos. I grew up the hard way because I went against expectations. Not every door was open, and some were slammed in my face. Today, I can claim my knowledge as my own. It was not given or handed down to me. I had to fight for it as an adolescent and a young woman. I had to figure out things out for myself. But by so doing, I am able to claim it and pass it on.

Moonglow

Jim is sitting at a picnic table with a crowd of guffawing male classmates at the noonday barbecue, the last of three days of my fiftieth high school reunion. I sit next to Sam at the opposite side of our host and classmate's backyard. Holding a bottle of lukewarm water, I feign interest in burial options for my husband and me with Sam, owner of the local funeral home. What I really want to do is talk to Jim.

Closing my eyes behind my sunglasses, I let my head rest on the back of my chair, lifting my face to the afternoon sun. The summer air smells of grilled meats mingled with the slight odor of dust that settles on the field where my childhood friend Carol and I parked our cars. We had come back to our hometown for the reunion without our husbands. Mine was working weekends; hers had been eager to come but was not invited. The aromas are pleasant except for the faint stench of the cows grazing in the meadows beyond the redwood fence.

My lingering question is not how and where my husband and I will be buried, but why, after two dates, Jim never asked me out again. In the 1950s, I didn't ask such a question, as it would have revealed that I cared. Back then, part of my puzzlement had to do with why Jim continued to flirt with me at Student Council meetings and school dances when we were both going steady with other people. Once, at a school dance, while walking past me and my boyfriend, Jim, escorting his steady, leaned close enough to whisper for my ears only, "I love my wife, but oh, you kid." The comment was the title of an old song my parents danced to about regret for lost love and a potentially two-timing husband. I remember thinking, *Am I encouraging this comment? And what, for heaven's sake, does he mean by this?*

In high school, it was this type of perplexity that I would confide in Carol. She suggested, "Jim prefers blondes. And besides, you and Steve are so cute together. And he's smarter than Jim, and an upperclassman."

"But he's not as good-looking as Jim, or an athlete, unless you count golf," I said. We agreed, except for the golf part, as her mom was a golfer of some repute.

At the time, I wondered why Jim still flirted with me. But when Carol reminded me that there was a bigger world out there after high school, I was more intrigued than puzzled. Carol had lived in Europe in the fifth grade, the year before we became best friends. I knew she was worldlier than I. The farthest I had traveled was with my parents to Uncle Jim's ranch some ninety miles north over two mountains on a narrow, switchback road.

I knew this barbecue would be my last chance to talk with Jim that weekend. I had seen him the night before at a private cocktail party for the elite athletic classmates and their wives. Carol and I were the exceptions.

Jasmine infused the air as nightfall pursued dusk. A holly hedge surrounded the outdoor area, dwarfing the juniper and maple trees, except for one mature oak. A grape arbor, installed with a mist cooling system, partly shaded the flagstone patio. The lawn, without a hint of dandelions, looked as if it had been rolled out that day. A Mahoney bar was set with long-stemmed wine glasses, bowl-shaped for red wine, and tulip-shaped for white. An ice bucket filled with bottles offered the promise of chilled wine.

Our host, John, the former star quarterback, was still handsome and youthful looking, having kept his muscular physique and his full head of hair, unusual in this crowd of former football stars. His home, on what had once been a chicken farm, was of redwood and natural stone from the area and worthy of a spread in *Architectural Digest*. The potential article would be complete with a photo of his second wife, thin, beautiful, and twenty years younger, who was impeccably dressed in a short, chocolate-brown linen dress.

With our glasses of chilled pinot grigio, Carol and I joined Jim and half a dozen former jocks. They were teasing him about being named "Mr. Hometown" in a recent article in the city's newspaper.

Our host, the former quarterback, said, "Nice picture, Jim, but what was with that Most Valuable Player trophy? Did you steal it? When are you going to give it back?"

Jim still had his good looks, though no longer an athletic body. He had been Cary Grant handsome, strikingly tall with dark eyes, black hair with a hint of sideburns on his smooth face, and broad shoulders that had accentuated his narrow waist and hips. Jim had been known for being outgoing, popular, and polite, often funny but not at the expense of others. I had never known him to be crude or drunk. Seldom had I heard him talk about himself, and he never bragged about his accomplishments. I would learn the next day from the Mr. Hometown article that he had been most valuable player in All-League, outstanding lineman and High School Hall of Famer for football and track.

Now Jim is bulky. His middle is as broad as his shoulders. When he moves, he stoops slightly and lumbers with a limp.

As we face each other, I realized what had initially endeared this man to me might have been his good looks and his athletic abilities, which had now faded. But what was unchanged were his penetrating eyes, humble good humor, and generous smile.

I venture, "Tell us more about the Mr. Hometown article."

"Well, it was a surprise. I didn't know what to say about my life, you know. And there was a lot I wouldn't say," he adds, laughing. Looking down at the grass, he says, "I'm really honored and embarrassed."

"I'd like to see the article," I say.

He promises to bring me a copy later that night at the dinner dance, where he will be giving the welcoming address as emcee and former class president.

As we sip our chilled wine, Carol and Jim begin talking about their children and grandchildren's athletic activities. My thoughts drift back to our first date.

We had gone to a school dance in the gymnasium and danced every dance to a four-piece male band with a girl singer, all students from our high school. I remembered how he took my hand and led me to the floor, turning toward me with a smile and inviting eyes that made me blush. I was thrilled to be the center of his attention. With his hand touching the small of my back, he gently drew me close until my head rested on his muscular chest. I raised my hand to his shoulder as the space between us narrowed, and I felt his chin touch my hair. He did not hum or sing the words to "Moonglow." That would have broken the spell unless he could have sung like Frank Sinatra. But the lyrics, "We seemed to float right through the air," described how I felt in his embrace and moving together with the rhythm of the music.

After a slow drive home, Jim opened my car door and walked me to the front door. Mom, as usual, was knitting in her chair in the living room, facing the street with a view through the large window to our long driveway. It was her habit to keep a vigil until her three daughters came home from their dates. Jim and I said goodnight beneath the front porch light. We did not kiss, which was the family's expectation: Never kiss on the first date. Fortunately, we had a second date.

The voice of our host, John, cuts into my reverie and brings my focus back to the cocktail party. With a chuckle, he says, "I have a seventeen-year-old son that I still have to put through college."

Jim, in his baritone voice, says in a teasing way, "Don't talk to me about seventeen-year-olds. I've already put three kids through college, and now I have a grandson that age."

The laughter of the crowd, like the wine, is full-bodied, with a touch of cattiness and an aroma of envy that stays with us as we depart for the dinner dance.

Now at the barbecue, I am sitting here listening to Sam drone on about burial options.

"Do you want to be cremated?" Sam asks.

"I'm not sure," I reply. "My Catholic instruction still haunts me. Nana was cremated, but she was Methodist, I think. She didn't go to church."

I am sweating in a hip-hugging, black linen skirt and tiny tank top, squeezed next to Sam. By this third day of events, my sparkle is fading, but not my A-list red pedicure peeking out of my apple-green sandals with heels that lift my height and spirits. I can stride with confidence when the time comes to move.

"It's all about economics, nothing else," Sam pontificates. "The Catholic Church has changed. But it's all about economics. If you want your husband with you, that will be another two-fifty."

When I explain that my husband's family has a large plot in his hometown's cemetery and wants to be cremated and buried there, Sam comes up with an alternative plan. "Listen, you could both have some of your remains here and some there." And then with a mischievous grin, he adds, "But when the Revelation comes, I don't know what will happen."

The noonday heat is intensified by the lack of shade. Feeling the weariness of this three-day reunion, I get up to make my rounds, to thank the committee members and the hosts, with an eye toward saying good-bye to Jim.

Maneuvering around long benches, folding metal chairs, and crowded tables, I stop and say farewell to classmates. As I get closer to Jim, he turns toward me. In the bright sunshine, his dark eyes beneath black eyebrows are in striking contrast to his receding shock of white hair. I am captivated by Jim's broad smile. He sits squeezed into a patio chair between two eight-foot metal picnic tables. In this corner of the yard, there is no other place to sit and barely enough room to move, so I stand close to him, looking down. I'm not sure what to say. He says, "Thank you for coming to the reunion."

Taking his extended hand, I reply, "Thank you for bringing the newspaper article to me at dinner last night. I must say I'm impressed by how much you've done for the community and by your fondness for our town."

"Well, I guess I'm just a homeboy," he says softly. "You know, I did go away for two years in the service, but I came back. And then later I had an opportunity to work in a big city. I thought about it but decided to turn it down."

"It's nice to be that sure of yourself," I say, thinking about how satisfied I am that I'd left for college and never moved back.

As I am about to leave, I realize the mysterious end of our brief romantic past will remain unknown because of my hesitation to bring up the subject. It's as if I am reverting to my high school self, too timid to ask him directly why he stopped dating me. I say, "Well, I think it's time to say good-bye."

But Jim extends our conversation. "I'm the fourth generation of our family, and every generation worked and raised their families here. I love this town and the people and have no desire to live anywhere else."

Looking into his eyes, I think, *He actually did what was expected of him and with pride. I know it takes courage to leave, but does it also take courage to stay?*

All I manage to say is, "Well, it's been great to see you."

As I lean toward Jim for a hug, he grasps my arms gently and pulls me close. With piercing eyes and a bashful grin, he whispers, "I dated you in the tenth grade, and I loved you. And you dated Jerry Sowell and broke my heart."

Instantly I am aware of how I miss this feeling of being looked at with adoration. Once upon a time, my husband gave me that look, but it gradually faded like a stunning sunset. Then I begin to realize that this unexpected disclosure is the practical answer to the mysterious end of our high school dating. Surprised by his pronouncement, I start to pull away. "Oh! Ah, you know, well, you know, or it could have been Ted Price." Watching his smile disappear and his eyes, still intense but not as animated, my immediate thought is, *Why did I say that? Why didn't I tell him the truth, that Jerry was my best male friend but not a boyfriend?* But it's too late. Regret sticks in my throat like a fish bone.

I hear the sound of metal chairs scraping over the uneven cement floor as his friends attempt to discreetly move away from this tender but clumsy scene. The noise causes my gaze to drift momentarily from Jim's Irish eyes to the nearly empty whiskey bottle on the table and his two-inch smoldering cigar in the ashtray.

My eyes return to his. We are still holding each other's arms, his massive, covered in thick black-and-gray hair with an expansion-band wristwatch, and mine petite with practically no hair, but an abundance of age spots. *Is this my chance to apologize for my insensitive remark? Or to explain how disappointed I was that he never asked me out again? And that Jerry was a friend, not a boyfriend?*

As I open my mouth to say . . . something, Carol's thundering voice explodes with her contagious laughter. "Hey, Jim, thanks for smuggling that newspaper article to my buddy last night."

I straighten up and feel the strain in my lower back. "I didn't smuggle it; I gave it to her," he replies in a somber tone.

No one speaks. I look at Carol, she looks at me, and then we both look at Jim. It is obvious that Carol is not leaving my side. Ignoring her, I bend toward Jim for a good-bye hug. To my surprise we kiss on the lips. I'm not sure who initiated it. As I hug Jim, I feel his padded body brace under his loose-fitting shirt. Looking down as we slowly part, I am surprised to see his square kneecap showing beneath his shorts, from what I presume is knee replacement surgery. Looking into his eyes, I whisper, "Take very good care of yourself."

As Carol and I start walking together toward our cars to go our separate ways, I feel a need to digest what just happened with Jim. And I am not interested in dissecting it with Carol right now. I know, and I think she does too, that I will probably tell her another time what happened before she interrupted Jim and me.

As I get into my husband's convertible, I am thinking how reunions put me in a tricky state, because they are an occasion for remembering what I was and picturing what I might have been. I have current conversations, but I also reminisce about things that happened more than fifty years ago. And here's the tricky part: I imagine other versions of a life I did not live.

Driving away through the rolling hills of lush vineyards, I let reality wrestle with nostalgia as I remember leaning over and hugging this six-foot-two, heavyset man wearing a body brace, with crippled knees, twice divorced, and married to his third blonde wife. I think, *Could this declaration of love possibly have been fueled by alcohol?* Yet in my head I heard the lyrics, "I'll always remember that moonglow gave me you," I'll always remember the song, "Moonglow," that takes me back to my first love. Unlike reality, nostalgia is distilling. It simplifies memories and invites you to remember your youthful past through the gauzy lens of time. You imagine what might have been. Would you go back and make different choices? It's hard to imagine. But isn't it interesting that something that only lasted two dates could stay in your mind, forever perfect, untarnished by the things that make marriage long and muddled and complicated? My marriage that is decades long is muddled and so complicated that I can't be singular in my feelings.

I had an opportunity to see Jim again at our fifty-fifth high school reunion. He was sitting on an overstuffed couch, in the room between the smaller bar room and the larger dining room set up for dinner at the Elks' Club. Most of the alumni were in this room enjoying a before dinner drink. The hum of conversations made for an inviting atmosphere.

Jim's wife, Mary, was sitting on the arm of the couch, leaning over occasionally to remind Jim who was speaking to him. The word had spread that Jim had dementia, possibly Alzheimer's. People were saying what a shame it was because he had been known for his extraordinary ability to remember facts and people's names. Now Jim couldn't be left alone because he would wander away and not be able to find his way back. Mary had to give up her job to be his caretaker.

Classmates were coming to Jim to greet him. Carol was talking to him, and I was nearby talking to other people. Carol glanced up and motioned for me to come over, ever looking out for my best interests.

She moved away as I sat down on the couch next to Jim. I was again drawn to his inviting eyes. I drew close so he could hear me over the jovial sounds of classmates in the room. I said, "Hi Jim. It's Donna Brazzi. How are you?

His eyes grew brighter as he smiled. I don't know, but I think he might have recognized me. After he studied my face for some long moments, he said, "I dated you."

"Yes, we did date."

"Was I a gentleman?"

"Of course, you were, Jim. A perfect gentleman."

That was the last time I saw him, except at his funeral at St. Johns' Catholic Church, in Napa, our hometown. He had a full military escort, and bagpipes, as he was Irish. I will always remember moonlight and Jim.

They say that past memories are often the ones that stay as people age, even if they cannot remember everyday practical things. Seeing Jim again was a mixed opportunity of nostalgia for our high school romance and the reality that he may or may not have even recognized me. And it is sad to see how age can change a person's mind.

At times, I find myself remembering my first love, especially on warm summer moonlit nights. For the most part, what I miss more than the feeling that fresh hope of first love brings, is that life was filled with so many choices and possibilities. But that's my youthful self, wanting attention again. Yet, she can only be a memory.

Lifeguard Ken

I guess when you agree to marry a guy with a history of "heavy drinking," you should know what you're getting into. This was a guy who drove us off the edge of a windy road on the way home from a date one night, and yes, I should have known better. My only defense is that I was stupid in love with him in the summer of 1960.

That spring I had applied for, and been offered, a job as a waitress at Hoberg's Resort in Lake County, north of San Francisco. Ken was the lifeguard there, and this was supposed to be my liberation year, leaving home after college, but Mother resisted. She called Hoberg's Resort "the Pit of Sin." My sister Evelyn and I wondered how she knew this. No matter, because Mom flatly stated, "No daughter of mine is going to be waitressing and living there on her own."

I was twenty and would be graduating in June with an AA from Napa Junior College. In September I would be leaving home for UC San Francisco to study dental hygiene.

Defending my position to Mom that I could take care of myself proved useless. Securing Dad's support was critical as he was able to reason with Mom that her uncle, my Great-Uncle Jim's ranch, was less than four miles from the resort. And for evidence of my protection against "sin," Uncle Jim came to the resort daily bringing his horses and guides for the guests' trail outings. At night my cousin Jimmy checked IDs outside the upper bar you passed on the way to the outdoor dance floor. And furthermore, the sheriff, Ann Hoberg, niece of the owners, was responsible for keeping the peace in Lake County; she would also be "looking out for me." Hoberg's on Cobb Mountain was a very small community where everyone knew each other.

Mom reluctantly gave in but was not happy about it. I wasn't clear why she wanted to hang on to me. Looking back, perhaps the reason might have been that I was the last of her three daughters, and the most anxious to get out of our small town and into the larger world, even though that summer world was a mere fifty-five miles away.

It was a thrill to be on my own, barring my own family bodyguards. However, my protectors also earned me respect with the resort owner, his son, and many longtime workers from the area who knew my relatives.

My roommate, Lyn, was a senior at San Francisco State, a year or two older than I and more experienced in just about everything. This was her second summer working at Hoberg's, and she knew everyone from the busboy to the owner, George, and his son, George Junior, my boss, who ran the dining room. She was the one who taught me how to carry the metal tray loaded with entrees on my shoulder without spilling au jus on the guests or myself. In addition, she warned me not to piss off the cook by asking for an end cut of prime rib, the Saturday dinner special.

Our schedule was a dream, starting at seven thirty for breakfast and finishing by eleven in the morning. There was plenty of time to swim in the afternoons before serving dinner at five. We got off at about nine o'clock, after which we'd quickly shower and change and dance the night away.

The resort was one of the largest in Lake County. The summer months were warm during the day, and at an elevation of 3015 feet, cool at night. The resort had been built in the 1930s, and in its heyday in the forties it had big name bands such as Tommy Dorsey, Harry James, and Xavier Cugat. The Hoberg's Pine Bowl dance floor was open to the stars and enclosed by a cathedral of pine trees.

In my time working at the resort, the clientele were families who came for a two-week vacation. They would sit at assigned tables with the same waitress, so it was easy to get to know them and their preferences. It was a pleasant association.

For the guests, there were two tennis courts as well as Ping-Pong, horseshoes, horseback riding, and a recreation room for cards. A beauty salon, originally built in the thirties, was open by appointment. The lower bar was open day and night, and the coffee shop fountain served from lunchtime until after the dance floor closed. The resort was a lot like the one portrayed in the movie *Dirty Dancing,* only without the dirty dance movements.

Lifeguard Ken was a "Hoberg." His mom and dad had met at Hoberg's in the thirties, which made our story of meeting at Hoberg's a family legend.

During the first weeks of my job that summer, Ken's fraternity brother Dick was visiting me for the weekend. Both were seniors at UC Berkeley. Dick was from my hometown. We had dated during my two years of junior college. On this particular date at Hoberg's, he made it his duty to point me out to Ken, saying, "Keep an eye out for Donna and take good care of her. It's her first time away from home." This gave me something I did not want, another protector.

My free time focus was to be at the pool, swimming and sunbathing while visiting with Lyn and other people I'd befriended at the resort, including Ken's aunt Marilyn, her young daughters, and Sal Carson's wife and their two young girls. Sal and his family, along with his ten-piece band, spent the season at the resort from Memorial Day to Labor Day. At night I loved the dancing, sometimes with friends who would come from Napa for the weekend, or with some of the staff members.

During the day, Ken and I ignored each other, except that he was watching me and the other young women at the pool while I was trying not to watch him. He was handsome and tanned, looked fit in a bathing suit, and drove a green sports car, an MGB convertible. I never saw him at staff meals. I learned later that he also taught private swimming lessons around the county. But he was always at the dances and was a very good dancer. Along with the other male employees, he was expected to dance with the women guests. But he and I had time to dance, and he taught me the cha-cha-cha and nothing more.

Toward the middle of summer, I invited my sister to join me for the weekend. To ensure that she would have a good time, I wanted her to have a dance partner. Without hesitation, knowing he would agree, I asked Ken, "Would you accompany me to the dances this weekend when my sister is visiting?"

"Yes, of course," he said.

"And could you invite one of your nice, polite fraternity brothers to be her escort?"

Ken's fraternity brother Ron was very polite, and my sister enjoyed herself. Everything went as planned, except that I fell in love with Ken, and the feeling was mutual. After that weekend we danced each night, went on occasional walks between shifts, and always checked in with each other.

Toward the end of our summer, Ken invited me to Sunday dinner at his home fourteen miles away, in Kelseyville. I was greeted with a hug from his mother, Marian, a big smile and firm handshake from his stepfather, Bill, and embarrassed giggles from his brother, David, who'd just graduated from high school and was soon off to Cal Poly in San Luis Obispo. His younger sister, Elaine, was quiet, but I was aware of her watching me throughout the meal. We sat at the dining room table and had Bill's special fried chicken. Marian told me years later how much they liked me right away at that dinner.

On the last night of our summer jobs, we agreed to meet before sunrise at a predetermined time and place. Sitting on a boulder, we watched the sun clear Cobb Mountain. I don't remember what we talked about, but I do remember two things. First, I loved our summertime together, and second, I wasn't ready to settle down.

In mid-September of 1960, my dad drove me to UC San Francisco and carried my possessions into the new Millberry dorms. It was not a tearful good-bye. With my enthusiasm and a great tan, I was thrilled to be on my own, with twelve female classmates and hundreds of dental, medical, and pharmacy students, almost exclusively men. All had bachelor's degrees, and many were returning veterans on the GI Bill.

Carol was my roommate, and Betty and Jill our suitemates. The living situation was pure fun. My classmates were bright and hardworking, and we shared our schedule of classes from eight to five. On Friday nights, several of us gathered regularly in our room while my suitemates played guitars. We sang, and some drank beer, enjoying letting go and sharing stories of school, dates, and other interesting topics.

Classes, on the other hand, varied. The basic sciences with about a hundred dental students were rote memorization, interesting but not intellectually challenging. The dental hygiene lectures were minimally challenging to boring. Our technique labs were not technically difficult, but a necessary part of preparation for seeing patients in the clinic toward the end of our junior year. I longed for a more challenging intellectual experience.

Back in high school in the late fifties, I had set my sights on medical school. But I was told by my counselor, "My dear, women who become doctors do not marry or have children." Unbelievable as that may seem, this was the era prior to the feminist movement. And being of Swiss–Italian descent, I knew I wanted eventually to be a wife and mother. But not before I achieved my economic and professional independence.

Upon graduating from high school in 1958, I had received honors as well as acceptance and a scholarship to UC Berkeley, but Mom forbade me to go. She threatened to send the police after me if I went. There was no challenging her on this. Dad, with his eighth-grade education, compared to Mom's high school, was no match for her stubbornness. Was it fear of my living in an urban area? Was it fear of losing her third daughter? Was I upsetting the family cultural norm since my two sisters had gone to the junior college? Did Mom think that I considered myself "better than" my sisters and the family tradition? Did Mom think it was inappropriate or arrogant of me to aspire to a four-year college degree?

Though I was ready to defy my mother, the police were another matter. So, I began my freshman year at the junior college, living at home for two more years before my liberation. I was unhappy and miserable and hid it during the day, but I let it show at home.

My part-time job, considered a plum, was working for the president of the board of trustees of the junior college, a dentist. He influenced and encouraged me to apply to UC San Francisco in dental hygiene. Of the potential occupations for women with science backgrounds in early 1960s—nursing, physical therapy, and dental hygiene—I chose the latter. Of course, there were women studying medicine, law, and other professions, but not many. According to the National Center for Education Statistics, the number of women in medical school in the United States in 1960 was 5.8 percent; in law school there were 3.7 percent women.

In my hometown of Napa with a 1960 population of 22,000, of whom merely 6 percent had four years or more of college, I knew no women doctors or lawyers. In short, I had no women role models.

In the fall of my first year at UC San Francisco, I received a call from Ken on the dorm hall phone. This was the first time we'd spoken since summer. He invited me to go to the Saturday football game and attend his fraternity party afterwards.

I was momentarily silent before I answered.

"Ken," I said, "thank you for the invitation, but I have a lot of studying to do. I don't think I will have time to be dating you."

Was I guarding my independent life from Lifeguard Ken? Because my true reason for saying "no" was that I knew I loved him, but in the sixties culture, the assumption was that women who married were usually expected to drop out of college and became wives. I was single-minded in my determination that I would not give up my long-awaited freedom. Besides, I wanted to be free to date others and enjoy the social part of my new college experience.

That rejection of his invitation ended my starry-eyed summer romance.

We lost touch after that. Occasionally I heard from a friend that Ken was studying to be a minister, which surprised me. He was living in Edinburgh, Scotland, and attending seminary. My friend had dated Ken prior to his leaving the country and said, "He's nice but too short for me."

Following my graduation in 1962, I flew to Hawaii to be a public health dental hygienist on the Big Island. Upon my return a year later, I was asked to join the dental hygiene faculty at UC San Francisco.

Toward the end of my two-year stint as faculty at UCSF, I dated a Midwestern man whom I had met at a dental conference on the East Coast. It was a long-distance relationship that became an engagement after a year. None of my family or friends liked him. He was divorced, or so he told me. He was a liar, and when I found out he was living with his wife and two daughters, I ended the relationship. He called me once after that and I slammed the phone down saying, "Don't ever call me again!" In retrospect, the relationship was an unpleasant episode in my life.

I changed my lifestyle in 1965 when I went from teaching at UCSF to full time private practice. I moved out of my single apartment in San Francisco to a shared apartment in a small town south of Berkeley. Leaving behind hours of teaching, lecture preps, and meetings, I enthusiastically embraced an abundant social life without wanting a serious relationship. I was twenty-five years old.

Jane, my roommate, and I regularly gave parties with wall-to-wall friends in our living room. Her dad was generous and bought the case of champagne we chilled in the bathtub filled with ice. We had two menus: hot dogs and champagne, or red wine and beef stroganoff. Our dessert was always the same, chocolate mousse decorated with whipped cream and made with Jell-O chocolate pudding. The presentation was impressive on a pedestal cake plate which we borrowed from Jane's mom.

We were single and happy. Two heads were better than one, sharing our own dating experiences and giving each other advice. We considered ourselves too clever by half about men, but we were perhaps too cocky about our joint skills.

About a year into this unattached carefree life, I was surprised by a phone call from Ken. He had returned from Scotland and was living close by in Orinda, the assistant youth minister of the Community Church. After a brief catch-up conversation, he said, "I'd like to take you out to dinner on Friday."

I said, "That would be nice, except I'm flying to Pasadena this weekend to visit some friends for a spring concert."

"How about lunch tomorrow?" he said.

"Okay. Come by my office about noon. I'll need to be back for a one o'clock patient."

Though I was surprised that he had found my phone number—I had moved twice since our last conversation five years before—it seemed appropriate that he should reenter my life at this time. Now that I was twenty-five, my parents had stopped asking me if I was going to marry, a sure sign in their eyes that I was headed for spinsterhood. Their feelings on the matter held enough sway that I started to consider I might be arriving a little late to the party. So I was pleased but cautious, with a feeling that fate might have a hand in this reunion.

I have no clear recollection of that meeting, except sitting across from him in my white uniform and shoes, and he looked as handsome as ever in khaki slacks and a short-sleeved white dress shirt, clean shaven with a butch haircut. We set a date for dinner the following Friday. I was interested but still somewhat skeptical about being in a relationship. I'd been distrustful about men since my engagement and the unpleasant aftermath. Ken's reentry in my life was a bit unsettling in some ways.

On our subsequent dinner date, a week later at a French restaurant in Sausalito, overlooking the San Francisco skyline, I seemed emotionally right back at Hoberg's. Or it might have been the brandy Alexander and bottle of red wine we polished off with dinner. We may even have had an after-dinner drink. My usual was a grasshopper. As we sat in his MGB sports car at my apartment, we immediately became passionate, as if the valve had been released on the pressure cooker. I felt we were in danger of going too far, and someone had to control this situation. Reluctantly, that was my job.

The next morning, I called him and said, "Ken, I don't think we should see each other again. Last night was too much too soon. I'm not ready for this."

He said, "It might have been the drinking. I promise we can take it slow. Because I would very much like to see you again."

I continued to date him, but not exclusively. However, within months we began seeing each other every week. He had another relationship with a girl in San Jose, which he ended, but the way he did it was not impressive. He simply never called her again.

Midway through our second year of exclusive dating, he drove us off the edge of a windy road on the way home from dinner and dancing. At one turn, the front wheel went over the edge, and thankfully it stopped, either because it was caught, or because Ken braked. We both got out of the car, thankfully not hurt. But I was scared of what might have happened, and I thought how stupid of me not to recognize the danger of being in a car with a drunk driver.

Ken's brother came to our rescue. He drove me home first. As he walked me to my door, his brother said, "Donna, I am so thankful neither of you were hurt. But this is not your problem."

Love might be blind, but it can also be foolish. In retrospect, it was absurd that I dismissed Ken's drinking as not being my problem. If I was going to be part of his life, it *was* my problem. I decided to stay in the relationship. I knew he was a "heavy drinker." The idea that he was an alcoholic was not something I contemplated or confronted. Unfortunately, this would not be the first time he put the two of us in danger due to his drinking.

Ken and I dated exclusively for close to two years. Gradually I became involved in the church where he worked and routinely joined him at the youth group gatherings on Sunday nights. In the first year of our renewed relationship, Ken asked me to accompany him as a chaperone with three other married couples and fifty teenagers for a week to an orphanage in Tijuana, Mexico. I was also to be the designated first aid person. We would travel by bus to the orphanage where we would be staying to assist the owners, Mr. and Mrs. Irwin Ford, and care for the orphans.

It was a challenging and life-changing trip for me. I had treated patients from all walks of life in the dental hygiene clinic at UCSF. I had volunteered my services in a free clinic in Berkeley. But I had never lived in a poor community.

Ken's kindness, organization, and dedication to helping others impressed me. I admired his ability to handle unexpected situations, like lack of water for baths, solved by taking the teenagers and orphans to the beach for an outing. Our focus was caring for and being with the children and monitoring how the teenagers were processing their experiences.

I was falling more in love with this guy. Our relationship was deepening. We shared similar values. My family and friends liked him and were happy for me and us, and his family felt the same. Yet we never talked about marriage. Call me old-fashioned, but it was up to the man to initiate the subject of marriage. It would have been inappropriate, or so I thought, for me to bring it up. But I was hopeful for a proposal.

But by December 1967, I was wondering if the nearly two-year commitment was a good investment in my future. I was twenty-seven. And then something happened to make me change my lifestyle again and stop waiting for him. Ken informed me that we would not be sharing Christmas together with his family, as we had done the previous year, along with all the other holidays. Because his brother-in-law was coming home from the Vietnam War, it would be an important time for his family, and Ken thought the homecoming might be awkward for his brother-in-law. Ironically, I was invited to go the airport with his family to welcome the returning soldier, and then to dinner afterward at his brother and wife's home, but not to celebrate Christmas.

It hurt to be excluded by him as not being "part of the family." Or, I wondered, *was he getting cold feet about us?* I cried on my sister's shoulder, had a long discussion with a male best friend, and decided to take action.

Within a day or two, I called up my college roommate, Carol, and invited myself to spend the first week of January at Sun Valley, Idaho, an exclusive ski resort. She was happy to have my company. That week improved my skiing and my attitude. I had a wonderful time on the slopes, in the hot tub, and on the dance floor, in that order.

Returning home, I felt an obvious chill from Ken. He picked me up from San Francisco airport. We were expected for dinner at his aunt and uncle's home in Burlingame where his uncle gave me a bigger hug and kiss than Ken did. I noted that. We continued to date, but not exclusively on my part. I began dating other men and was enjoying my renewed single life. No more waiting around for a proposal.

Over the next few months, Ken and I were developing a more argumentative relationship that culminated one night in a huge quarrel. The next day I felt I had been too combative and stopped by his office on my lunch break to make amends. I interrupted a meeting with Roger, a mutual friend of ours, who graciously left immediately.

Ken beat me to an apology that relieved the situation. It seemed both of us wanted our relationship after all. He asked if we could go out that night, and I agreed. As I left to go back to work, I felt better. I had some thinking to do about the way I had expressed my anger the night before.

Our date turned out to be a soccer game, which seemed curious to me. It was my first such event, but I could enjoy it. What was more curious was the way Ken was acting. He paid more attention to me than the game, held my hand throughout, and agreed with everything I said. I was intrigued because I knew how much he loved sports.

After the game, we went to the Claremont Hotel in Berkeley for a drink. The lounge had a view of the San Francisco skyline. We frequently came here for dancing and cocktails on Friday nights. But this was a Tuesday, and there was no dancing. After we ordered a cocktail and chatted about this and that for a while, Ken got out of his chair and down on one knee.

"Donna, I have known you and loved you for some time now. I admire the way you relate to people, and how caring you are in your work and with the teenagers at church," he began.

It seemed fairly predictable what was coming next, but also obvious that he had rehearsed his speech.

After a few more flattering sentences, Ken said, "Oh, darn. Donna, will you marry me?"

I was grinning so wide that it was hard to form the words to reply.

After a moment, he said, "Well, will you?"

"Yes, of course I will."

Ken ordered champagne, and we were hugging, toasting each other, and grinning like we had won the lottery. He suggested a long relationship should have a short engagement. Both of us agreed that the wedding should take place as soon as we could plan it. We set it for September, three months away.

We called my parents first, and then his brother and wife, then my sister Evelyn and her family. All were very happy for us. We decided to savor our experience and postponed telling his mom until we could be with her in person.

She happened to be in San Francisco visiting a friend.

The next day, we met her for lunch at the Iron Horse on Maiden Lane, "the place to be and to be seen." Between cocktails and ordering lunch, Ken lifted his glass and said, "Mom, I asked Donna to marry me, and she said yes."

Marian was so thrilled she practically vaulted out of her seat in this crowded, fashionable restaurant. Her joyful reply was, "It's about time."

I glowed at the comment.

In the end, Lifeguard Ken didn't save my life, but he offered a life together in marriage that could complement my independence. It was what I had been hoping for, but wasn't willing to wait forever.

It's Raining, and
I Married an Alcoholic

It's raining, and I married an alcoholic. While sitting at my desk, I watch the liquid tears fall from the sky. Outside my window, the nasturtiums are collecting water on their saucer-sized leaves. The new cedar fence that separates our property from the Johnstons' looks darker when wet. And the clothesline poles are soldier straight, while the lines play double Dutch in the wind.

We were in our late twenties when we married forty-seven years ago. It was obvious that Ken was a "heavy drinker." This was not unusual in the late sixties when there was a customary cocktail hour before dinner, when wine was not even considered a cocktail drink.

The smell of gin still puts me off. It's the smell of sadness. There were times when Ken was a functioning alcoholic. He never missed a day of work. There were other times I would choose to forget. Like the evening when we were leaving a church potluck at the Peterson's, and my husband urinated at the curb just past their house. This struck me as appalling behavior, and

I feared that other people from the church might see him. I felt that I needed to protect him and his reputation as minister.

There was another time in Scotland at John Muir's birthplace when he left the table to go to the bathroom. We could hear him heaving. Upon his return, Ian, our host, inquired about his health, and my husband explained that he had a "sensitive stomach."

I believed this explanation until he berated me, and thereafter, I found it hard to accept. When I brought up the subject of his drinking, he would often lash out at me. In the heat of an argument, he might shout, "Well, why don't you get rid of all the liquor in the house." I tried that. It didn't work. I learned later that he would stop at bars after church meetings. And then there were those many times he threw up at home, no longer bothering to blame his "sensitive stomach." With each passing year, there were more and more clues.

My husband was so likeable and, for Christ's sake, doing God's work. No one wanted to think he was an alcoholic—not his mom, his family, my family, or the congregation who all saw him drunk at functions but perhaps didn't notice since he was always pleasant in public. If they did suspect, they never brought it up. Only Bonnie, the organist and choir director, seemed to acknowledge it by slipping Ken breath mints on Sunday morning while she practiced before the service.

My denial was in part based on my lack of knowledge of alcoholism. The only alcoholic I knew was Judy's father. When she and I became best friends in the fifth grade, her father had left their family. The one time I saw him, Judy and I were in high school, walking down First Street in the middle of the day. As we rounded the corner of the pharmacy, a man in dirty, rumpled clothes lay in the gutter in front of the bar. I had never seen this before and thought he was asleep. Judy whispered, "Donna, that's my dad," and we walked on without stopping. I was stunned. I felt so sorry for my best friend. The people I knew, including Judy, never talked about alcoholism. If I overheard adults discussing it, they defined it as a moral failure to control consumption. In my adult mind, an alcoholic was a man in the gutter.

When I was a new bride, I couldn't—or perhaps refused to—see the clues. In part, I probably did not want to. I was trying to protect his public image in the church, after all, and our families and friends. I also was protecting my public persona and our marriage.

One night in December, five years into our marriage and seven months pregnant with our daughter, my illusions were shattered. My husband and I were returning home from a Christmas party. Ken was driving on the freeway when a police car stopped us just short of our turnoff. It was cold and raining lightly. The officer leaned in to ask Ken for his driver's license and car registration. In the next moment, I watched as my husband attempted to walk a straight line, without success. The officer then asked me to get out of the car and walk the line. I was indignant that he suspected a pregnant woman of being drunk. My indignation quickly turned into pity for my husband, as I watched him get handcuffed, and the officer's hand on his head as Ken was shoved into the back seat of the patrol car. There was only a brief moment to say good-bye through a partially opened window. "Call Nick," is the only thing he said. The patrol car pulled away. My last glimpse of my husband was him slumping in his seat with his head down.

Sitting by myself in the car, I was mortified yet trying to think rationally. Wiping tears from my eyes and taking a deep breath, I started the car. The rain was coming down hard now. I whispered to our unborn baby, "We are safe. It will be all right." As I was driving home to call Nick, it dawned on me that the officer had been concerned for my ability to drive home safely. I should have been more grateful.

It was after midnight when I walked into our home and was greeted by Angel, our basset hound, as if nothing had happened. Nick answered the phone on the first ring. He was a friend in his twenties, ten years our junior, who would have done anything for Ken. Nick was working for a group of churches, including ours, doing community work as his alternative service as a conscientious objector to the Vietnam War. We frequently had him for dinner to help supplement his meager salary. Nick had also stayed with us when he got the chicken pox.

He was at our front door in less than twenty minutes. He knew what to do. I certainly did not. He drove us to an all-night bail bonding agency that was in a part of town I had previously avoided. In the dark, with the rain coming down in sheets, the street looked threatening. The only other storefronts were bars and one coffee shop. The bondsman delivered the necessary paperwork for Ken's release after we filled out forms and paid the price. How we got the cash, I don't remember. But I do recall that I had difficulty looking this character in the eye.

It took about an hour to reach the county jail. Nick and I traveled mostly in silence. The brightly lit waiting room was crowded, and it took a while before my husband emerged carrying his shoes. It was painful to see his tears and to hear his repeated apologies. He did not want me to hug him. He said, "I'm not worthy. You don't want to touch me." For him, it was a humiliating experience, but it propelled him to begin his recovery journey. Shortly after his arrest, Ken attended his first AA meeting and took up jogging in place of the cocktail hour. For this I was utterly grateful.

Our daughter was born on the first day of spring. I had never known such joy, and I felt Ken's happiness too. His mom and dad came down from Lake County to help us when we arrived home from the hospital. Ken's grandmother had sent money that we used to buy a movie camera to record our first outing as a family. My mother-in-law needed no directions; she did the cleaning, washing, and gave our daughter her first bath while I watched. Ken's dad did the cooking during the time they stayed with us. He brought steaks to barbeque and Cold Duck, a pink sparkling wine my father-in-law always reserved for special occasions. My husband did not drink any. He hadn't touched alcohol since his arrest, and I was thankful for his two months of sobriety.

Eight years after Ken's arrest, he was called to a new congregation, and we moved, enrolling our daughter in the first grade, a two-block walk from our new home. Ken had not publicly disclosed his recovery, nor was it necessary.

When our daughter was in middle school, she called us to come pick her up from her first party. During the ride home she was upset and talked about not wanting any part of it, especially seeing her friends drinking and throwing up. Ken, in an impromptu disclosure, acknowledged his former drinking to her and said, "Sometimes I had trouble with drinking."

About two years later, Ken decided he wanted to tell the congregation. Prior to his disclosure. he told both me and, separately, our daughter of his decision. From the pulpit, after his sermon in Sunday service, he said, "I have something to announce" and momentarily lost his composure. The words were stuck in his throat. On the third try, he said, "I am a recovering alcoholic. And today I celebrate fourteen years of sobriety."

The majority of the congregation embraced him for his courage. Some said, "I wondered why you didn't drink." A few thought he should have kept that information to himself.

From the beginning of his recovery, I supported Ken attending AA meetings and having a sponsor, but I let him down by not going to Al-Anon meetings when he asked me to.

I was reveling in being a new mother and hated to leave our daughter any more than I had to. In retrospect, this was unfair to Ken and showed my reluctance to be more informed about his journey. Looking back, however, I feel I made the right choice for me and our daughter by focusing on how to mother her. Perhaps I could have learned to mother and partner with my husband in his recovery. I will never know. But I know I am not proud of myself for letting him down.

Ken celebrates his years of sobriety based on the year our daughter was born. And for his continuing, one day at a time, to remain clean and sober, I am so proud of him.

Much Ado about Something

I was scheduled to go into labor the next day at San Leandro Memorial Hospital, about twenty-five minutes north of our home in Hayward, California. My husband and I had been married for five years and now lived in the parsonage, part of his compensation as the minister of the Congregational Church of Hayward. The ranch-style home was nondescript with four bedrooms and one bath, a front lawn, and a backyard with a brick patio and a playground-size swing set. It was much larger than our previous Arts and Crafts-style, one-bedroom flat in the Berkeley hills overlooking the Claremont Hotel that had been mine before we were married. Our new home was in a tract development. I missed the architectural charm of the old place and the smell of baked goods from the hotel early in the morning.

When we moved to Hayward, after five months of marriage, we did not have enough furniture to fill the house, except for the kitchen and dining room. So our living room had a large beanbag chair and a fifty-gallon tank with saltwater fish that my husband had brought from his bachelor cottage. I brought a few lamps, a hand-me-down wooden couch with six pillows that my college roommate's mother had given me, and a round oak table with four chairs.

Faced with decorating, we shopped second-hand stores and managed to fill three of the four bedrooms. One was my husband's study. We purchased a massive desk, and I refinished it by stripping the paint and lovingly sanding and staining it, which turned out just okay considering the amount of time I put into it. But it served the purpose. One room was my sewing room/junk room. The third had my old double bed from my flat. That left our bedroom, the largest bedroom of all. Fortunately for us, a couple from my husband's former congregation had an antique Victorian bedroom set that included a four-poster bed, two chests of drawers, and a rocking chair that their adult children no longer needed. The bedroom set suited us quite well, and it is still in use forty-eight years later.

With childbirth, one usually doesn't know when delivery will start, unless it is a Caesarean section. But Dr. Gary, my obstetrician, determined that I was due or possibly overdue, so he scheduled me for an appointment to induce my labor at eight in the morning seven days past my due date. I trusted Dr. Gary as he had cared for me physically and emotionally through two previous miscarriages. He assured me that miscarriages were normal, and that I would certainly carry a pregnancy to full-term. I found this reassuring.

With my suitcase packed, my husband and I decided there was no reason why we shouldn't drive to the American Conservatory Theatre in San Francisco that night, about an hour away. We had season tickets, and we were looking forward to Shakespeare's *Much Ado About Nothing*. We figured if my water broke, we would still get to the hospital on time. Looking back, I see it was risky, but we were prepared. Just in case, we had put my suitcase, packed with all the hospital's recommended items, in the car.

Arriving at the Geary Theatre, we walked down the aisle and sat in our usual seats, next to my friend Jackie and her date. Jackie was a friend from college and a dentist with a solo practice in San Francisco. She was surprised to see us. "Donna, what are you doing here?" she asked. "What if you start labor?"

I tried to put her at ease by joking with her a bit. I said, "Remember our anatomy class? You did get an A in it, didn't you?"

If I went into labor, I hoped she would try to remain calm. With a nervous laugh, she said, "I do have dental floss with me, so I could tie off the umbilical cord."

As the curtain was rising, I said, "Relax, Jackie. Enjoy the play. It will be fine. Nothing's going to happen tonight."

I was excited to have my baby, despite being considered old for childbirth at age thirty-two in 1973. But my pregnancy had been uneventful, and I was healthy and had continued teaching and giving finals right up to the day before I was to deliver. It was a busy time as I prepared to take a leave without pay for six months. There was no such thing as a maternity leave then, but as the new mom I was eager to be, I was looking forward to my time at home with my baby.

As my husband drove me to the hospital the next morning, we were both excited, only to be told as we arrived at the fifth floor that all the rooms were full, and we should sit down and wait. I watched as nurses and doctors moved in and out of the four rooms. Dr. Gary stopped as he passed by, inquired about how I felt, and said, "It shouldn't be too long."

Within an hour or so, I was lying in a bed and prepped for childbirth. A needle in my arm was attached to a bottle of liquid hanging on a pole. I was also hooked up to a monitor that kept track of my contractions. Just as the nurse was about to start the drip to inject the medication to induce my labor, I started contractions. I took that as a good sign. My husband sat in a chair next to me and held my hand as we made small talk about the progress of the birth.

Every twenty minutes or so, Dr. Gary would come in and check on me and the monitor. My husband and I had requested that he be in the room during delivery. This was unusual at the time, but Dr. Gary allowed it. However, I found it peculiar that every time a nurse or Dr. Gary came in to examine me, my husband would be asked to leave.

I was ready and feeling happy. I was the center of attention with Dr. Gary and my husband looking at me from the posterior angle. Time passed quickly, and at 1:06 p.m., our daughter was born, presenting fist first, then head and body. Since it was the early 1970s, in the midst of the feminist movement, I claimed she was entering the world with her fist first as a sign of "power to the women," a part of the birth story that has remained family folklore all these years.

While the nurses tended to her, and Dr. Gary left to deliver more babies, I waited to meet our daughter. As the nurse laid this seven-pound, dark-haired baby girl in my arms, I was breathlessly in awe of her. She looked at me with such intensity, as if she had known me from a previous life.

With her birth, I found a deep well of wisdom from generations of mother, grandmother, great-grandmother, and beyond. Though I had read the popular book of parenting, Dr. Benjamin Spock's, *The Common Sense Book of Baby and Child Care*, I depended on my own intuition, and in time trusted my instincts with growing confidence in my abilities. There were times I almost wavered in my confidence, such as when my mother-in-law, who had been helping me for my first week at home, told me on the last day of her visit that I was to give our daughter her bath. I was uneasy about this, but with my mother-in-law by my side, I managed fine and regained some confidence.

As the years passed, I found such joy in mothering our daughter. It was a time of introspection, and dipping into this well of instincts, I followed my intuition from an innate trusting of my mothering abilities. However, when I returned to work after six months, there were times when managing my teaching, church, and family responsibilities left me wondering about my priorities. One Saturday sticks in my mind. I was rushing to go to a conference. My daughter, then six or seven, was at home with my husband who was working in his study. She sat in the beanbag chair in front of the TV watching cartoons, a regular Saturday morning event. I was late and rushing down the hall from our bedroom. On my way, I stopped to pull a comforter from the hall closet for our daughter. To my horror, out flew a litter of newborn kittens, with their mother giving me a lashing. I stopped long enough to put them back on another blanket, and to tell my husband and daughter that her cat, Mrs. Landa, had delivered kittens sometime in the night. I missed my daughter's delight in the new kittens as I hurried out the front door. At times like this, I felt guilty for leaving her. Guilt, as they say, is the gift that keeps on giving.

It was reassuring that our daughter's pediatrician, Dr. Ezekiel, responded to my doubts by saying, "If and when you do something wrong, Donna, don't worry. Monica knows that you love her." It would take three more decades before I fully embraced the extent to which this was true.

Each year for my daughter's birthday, amid the party decorations, cooking, and gift-wrapping, I took time to reflect and write her a birthday letter. I would write how much I loved her, how proud I was of her choices, and most of all, how much I admired her thoughtfulness and kindness to her friends, family, and everyone she interacted with. I was so pleased and gratified about her kindness because she emulated my dad's generosity of spirit, something I myself constantly worked on.

For my daughter's fortieth birthday, her husband invited family and friends to submit a handwritten note on a post-card or a one-page letter to Monica that he then scanned into an electronic photo album. He entitled the book *Forty*.

In my letter, I told her that when I gave birth to her, I was born to the woman I wanted to be. From her, I learned to take risks, by watching her at age five climb the pine tree that was as tall as our roof, outside our Hayward home. And when she was frightened, she had the guts to get herself down, guided by my husband's instructions.

I wrote in the letter how I had become more comfortable in the world of ideas by watching her in high school at the Lincoln–Douglas debates. In her freshman year, she supported my going back to graduate school. In my family, she alone understood why I was taking this risk.

My husband, on the other hand, was resistant to my desire for a change. I had said to him, "I am no longer challenged intellectually in my current teaching job. I need and want a new challenge and career."

He said, "Brother Lawrence made a meditation of doing the dishes. Try to consider doing that in your job."

My daughter did not question why I stayed up until two or three in the morning studying, whereas my husband would tell me I was not sufficiently well organized. When I expressed doubt that I would pass my qualifying exams, she reminded me how fortunate the university was to have me as a student. He told me he would still love me if I failed. My daughter was the one who encouraged me in supportive language when I had doubts, who gave me courage; when I was vulnerable, she gave me strength.

In my letter for her fortieth birthday, I wrote that she was my heroine who protected me one Friday night late on a crowded street in the West Village of Manhattan. She verbally took on seven young drunks because one of them bumped into me, spilling his drink. She shouted, "You do not bump into my mother and spill your drink on her without apologizing. You should be ashamed of yourself." With a few choice swear words, she gave him and his crowd a tongue-lashing, and they gave us a wide berth.

My daughter is an artist, and she called me an artist before I could take that mantle upon myself. She was relentless about pushing and supporting me as a writer. She and her boyfriend (now her husband) came to visit me at my first writer's residency. My daughter knew how important this residency was to me. They drove from San Diego to Washington and took the ferry to Whidbey Island. They had just graduated from college, with student loans, but the two of them presented me with a gift. As I untied the red satin ribbon and opened the small box, I was surprised and overwhelmed by their generosity. It was a figure of a woman in sterling silver holding a red jewel over her head, hanging from a sterling silver chain. At this and my other residencies, she would write to me regularly. On a third residency, I received a daily voicemail from her, reading a poem.

She wasn't born on the night of *Much Ado About Nothing*, but she's given me much ado about so much. I gave her life, and she's given me inspiration, the courage to take risks, and a relationship beyond belief.

Confessions of
a Minister's Wife

Being new to the small community of three thousand people in the hills of Berkeley in 1980 was constricting enough. I preferred the anonymity of a city. This unincorporated area we moved to was a village, much like the one in Angela Lansbury's *Murder She Wrote*, a TV series from the mid-eighties. Like Cabot Cove, Maine, our village had its own post office substation in the pharmacy, a grocery store, bank, and hardware store. Similar to Cabot Cove, gossip traveled fast. The only difference was that we didn't have a murder every week.

It was not possible for me to be incognito when I went for my daily run on the only street in and out of my new community. I had heard comments about other runners like, "I see her every day running, and she always seems unhappy," or "That runner has a funny stride." It did make me wonder what people might have been saying about me. I learned that any news would likely be reported in the community newsletter, such as a letter to the editor from a disgruntled neighbor complaining of another neighbor's loud music. It also printed announcements about fiftieth anniversary celebrations, church notices of meetings, choir practice, and social activities, elementary school science fair winners, and other newsy items.

I stood out for being "the minister's wife," though I saw myself as a professional woman. I was teaching dental hygiene at a community college in the primarily working-class city of Hayward where I'd lived for the past decade with my husband. It was where our daughter, now six years old, had been born. My students were a mixture of first generation, returning older, and younger women. Like them, I was first generation; my dad was an immigrant.

From an outward appearance, I was the type to fit into my village of an upper middle- class highly educated people. I was Caucasian with a married name of American pioneer descent. I had unearned status as the wife of the minister and the mother of a first-grader in one of the best elementary schools in the district. Like the women I met in the village, I had an above average public school education with a prestigious university degree. My manners and speech were more middle class than my working-class background might have otherwise suggested, thanks to my mother's insistence on proper public behavior and especially her use of and emphasis on correct English.

I joined the PTA board and volunteered in my daughter's classroom on Tuesday mornings at eleven. Sitting in the back of the classroom, I tutored the one African American first grader in reading. She came from what people referred to as "the flats," interpreted as not "the hills."

The monthly board meetings were serious business. The dozen board members designed and volunteered for the supervision and staffing of the library, the tutoring program, the crosswalk guards, and the biggest project, the annual carnival fundraiser. This was an all-day affair at the school on the Saturday before Mother's Day. There was a bake sale, silent auction, white elephant sale, plant sale, carnival, and barbecue lunch, cosponsored with the Dads' Club. The PTA mothers were proud to have traded their educational degrees for volunteer work for their children, church, and community.

Of course, women knew I worked, but I learned to keep a low profile about my professional life commuting an hour four days a week to Hayward but keeping Tuesdays available for volunteer work. If the subject of my work came up, the usual response was why the other woman had given up work for motherhood, so I learned not to mention it. I suspected that my situation—what was referred to as a "working mom" in my new community—did not fit the preferred role of stay-at-home mother of a young child. It was shades of the fifties in the eighties that left me feeling inauthentic in both the church and the PTA.

I met women who volunteered for PTA and church women in my new community. There were working women, but I knew them only through unflattering hearsay. One example was at a PTA board meeting when an agenda item requested volunteers for homemade baked goods for the Teacher Appreciation Tea. I listened as one member said, in a tone as bitter as lemon pie, "Call the working moms to provide the baked goods. And tell them no store-bought varieties. It's the least they can do."

I shrank in shame for not speaking up to defend the "working moms" and challenge the stereotype of the mothers who worked, women like me. I feared they would talk behind my back and taint me as one of those "working moms," so I remained silent. By keeping my work life and community life separate, I was safer from gossip, but I felt like a fake and a traitor.

Most of the people in the church knew I worked but generally ignored it. I felt the expectation of volunteering, so I sang alto in the church choir, leaving my daughter to sit alone or with other children in church until it was time to go to Sunday school. At various times, I also taught Sunday school, served on the board of deacons, worked on the Christmas bazaar and luncheon, and hosted the party of the Christmas carolers, the new members gatherings in the parsonage, and any other event where help was asked of me.

I enjoyed it for a while, until my daughter entered junior high. Then I decided to take myself seriously. After six years of PTA, I began to explore graduate school and taking a leave of absence from the church.

With this journey came my heightened questioning of the role of the minister's wife. Basically, I was fed up with it. Even more, I was mad at myself for the amount of time I had given to it and how long it had taken me to act. In addition, I asked myself how my life changes would affect our marriage. My husband did not discourage me from applying to graduate school, but he was not particularly supportive. Also, I feared how my being a full-time student and continuing to teach dental hygiene would affect our teenage daughter as she entered high school. These career changes would demand more of my time that could take away from my mothering. However, she was encouraging and overwhelmingly supportive, as I knew she would be.

It irritates me that there are traditional assumptions about the "minister's wife," the woman who, from my personal knowledge, is expected to be religious, devoted to her husband, his work, and his church. Because I was raised Catholic, I had little familiarity with what was expected of me when I married. Often, I was taken by surprise with congregational demands on my time, posed in questions such as "You will join the choir, won't you?" and "We need someone to teach the fourth grade in Sunday School. Will you do it?"

Despite these expectations, I initially enjoyed the small church we were associated with in Hayward, California, in the formative years of our marriage, pregnancy, and parenthood.

People in the church were generous and kind, happy to have a young couple as pastor and wife. Since we lived in a parsonage, people had freshly painted the house, and male volunteers were available to do home repairs. All this care and concern for our family also meant some loss of privacy. And I felt a responsibility to keep the parsonage, our home, tidy and presentable at all times, while teaching full time.

During the third year of Ken's ministry, I became pregnant for the first time. We were thrilled but had only told our families. During the Christmas season, I was taken by surprise when my husband announced from the pulpit, "And unto us a child will be born."

Before baby Jesus came to lie in the manger on Christmas Eve, my pregnancy ended in miscarriage. While hosting the annual Christmas carolers in the parsonage, I endured the congregants' kind words of concern, and too many personal stories of others' miscarriages. Why do people feel it is helpful to share their experience which is really never like one's own?

The following Christmas season. I had a second miscarriage that we kept a secret. With my third pregnancy, we went on vacation for a month to Maine to be with friends and to get far away. In due time, when the pregnancy continued and I began to show, the church people were very generous and gave me a baby shower. And when our daughter was born the following spring, the congregation was thrilled to be collective godparents. We also had plenty of teenage babysitters.

Even though the help was offered generously, I could not reciprocate, except by being actively involved in the church, something I saw as sinking into a deep hole of volunteerism. Also, we were being taken care of by others, without shouldering the responsibilities of homeowners. We didn't even pay our electrical bill; the church did, as they owned the property. Gradually the feeling of living under a patriarchal system felt more like a burden to me.

After thirteen years, we moved to another church and parsonage in Kensington, California, in 1980. I was still involved in the role of minister's wife, teaching Sunday school, singing in the choir, co-chairing the Christmas bazaar, and attending monthly deacon board meetings and several social functions. But after five years or so of getting very little out of worship, I attended church less and less often, and I ultimately stopped going altogether.

I clearly remember a time when my husband was the interim minister at a church in Marin County in Northern California in 2005. On the one occasion I did attend this church, for some reason I now cannot recall, Olle, a church member, approached me while I was in conversation with two other women. He was a tall Swede, close to retirement age but, like me, still employed.

Olle had kindly eyes and thin hair. I saw him coming toward me as he moved through a crowd of predominately white-haired women, in the Burlingame Fellowship Hall, named for a beloved, generous member who had since met her maker, as they say. Without waiting for his turn to speak, he greeted me with enthusiasm saying, "You're Donna, Ken's extension."

Experienced as I was from years in such social situations in my husband's churches, I thought before I spoke. I was attempting to keep my temper as I mentally envisioned punching this guy right in his smiling face. I thought to myself, *What do I have to lose? They could fire my husband, perhaps, or kick me out.* After forty years of these kinds of demeaning assumptions, I thought, *who cares?*

Reading his nametag, I said, "Olle, you might as well know something about me. I am a feminist, and I believe in equality." It felt good saying the words "feminist" and "equality" to him in a single sentence. Gauging his silence and observing him slumping slightly, I stood up taller, trying to ignore my rapid heartbeat. While speaking softly and gently, I added, "And I do not consider myself to be an extension of my husband." I gave Olle a big smile, like he was my new best friend.

He was startled. I waited in silence, resisting the temptation to rescue him with polite chatter. I was internally congratulating myself for having spoken kindly but firmly, and with integrity.

Olle said carefully, "All I meant is that you are here because of your association with him."

An A-plus response, though I suspected it was not entirely truthful. "I understand that," I replied.

In our marriage, when I was teaching dental hygiene, my husband was fond of saying to acquaintances and friends, "Donna saves teeth while I save the world." This attempt at a joke, at my expense, went on for too many years. Even after some private conversations with my husband, he couldn't seem to resist this line of banter. Once in London, in early repartee with two ministers, married to each other, I waited till the laughter subsided after Ken's "Donna saves teeth while I save the world." Then I said, "Honey, if you are saving the world, you are not having much success, what with war, disease, poverty, crime, racism, and homophobia." True, I shamed him publicly, but he never used that line again. And if he forgot and started to slip, my evil eye stopped him.

Where my professional job was concerned, being a "minister's wife" in one case was seen as an advantage. At my final interview and job offer in 1968 for teaching dental hygiene, I was told that being the minister's wife was in my favor, as I would be supervising women students. Is that why I got the job, on the assumption that I was a model of morality by association? This presumed advantage angered me more than it flattered me. Wasn't it my education, teaching experience, and clinical training that qualified me for the position?

While teaching in 2012 as a sociologist, a colleague asked me what my husband thought about churches being involved in civil rights activities while enjoying nonprofit status and paying fewer taxes. This male biologist and I were both recipients of the same federal funding for our research. Did he see me as a mouthpiece for my husband? How did he know my husband was a minister? I had never told him. Who did tell him and why?

Times are changing, fortunately. However, in my situation, I found that a minister's wife was expected to be self-sacrificing; if she had a job, it was secondary to her husband's work. This could be assumed of many women working in the early seventies, despite the emerging feminist movement. It wasn't that long ago that wives and mothers who worked outside the home were assumed to be doing so for additional income for home décor or family vacations. It was a strategy and justification for paying women less than men for an equivalent job. Women with careers were considered selfish if they were passionate about a job that, God forbid, interfered with their husbands' presumably more important work. In Ken's case, this was saving the world while saving souls from hell and damnation.

I assumed the role of minister's wife when we were married the year Martin Luther King Jr. was assassinated, and five years after Betty Friedan's *The Feminine Mystique* was published. Women's assumed roles in society were being challenged. I was making up my version of a minister's wife as I went along, and that evolved over the years from compliance to rebellion to nonparticipation.

During graduate school for my doctorate from 1989 to 1992, I used being in school and working as an excuse to take a leave of absence from the role of minister's wife. After I graduated, I came to recognize that it was time for me to quit the responsibilities that came with the role.

I even went so far as to release the minister's wife role in a ceremony with my closest female friends, my second feminist circle. First, I asked Pat, an educational specialist and wise spiritual woman, if she would design a feminist ritual to be held in my home. On the designated Sunday afternoon, six of us sat in a circle on a rug in my living room. The other women who attended the event were my walking partner, an author;

an attorney; a French teacher; and my daughter. Pat started by waving the smoking sage wand and spoke of cleansing the room and those in it of negativity, an ancient smudging ritual used by Native American cultures. I was generously supported and loved for my journey in releasing my traditional role and transitioning toward my more authentic self.

After formally leaving the role of minister's wife in 1992, I completed my transformation and resigned from teaching dental hygiene. The turning point came when I returned home from Hedgebrook, in late summer of 1995. This was ten years prior to Ragdale where I came clean about my two secrets.

Returning to my sociology teaching and research job at California State University Hayward, I relished the experience of freedom from keeping secrets about my past roles and returning to being my own boss. Employing graduate students as research associates offered me the opportunity to mentor three women into sociology doctoral programs and one man into medical school; he earned a double degree in medicine and public health. I continued to meet with women in Oakland, California; Rochester, New York; and Chicago, Illinois who lived with HIV/AIDS in secrecy, fearful of being labeled and stigmatized.

The long journey from two subservient roles to becoming my own person was accelerated by my decision to stop living with the accumulated mountain of anger, primarily at myself, and the culture that dictated and perpetuated women's stereotypic roles. I used that anger as fuel in reclaiming my younger self, the one who had the drive to leave the limitations of my hometown and eventually the confines of the cultural roles for women.

They no longer defined me.

A Surprising Grief

I was going to have a hysterectomy; that was clear. I'd had a biopsy that revealed cervical cancer, and there was no other option. And with the operation just days away, I was having a prickly time dealing with the prospect of having no more children. This shouldn't have been a big issue: our only child, a daughter, was in the sixth grade, my husband had had a vasectomy, and I was forty-four years old. As irrational as it seemed, I was fuming. I had shared my feelings with female friends and colleagues who, though sympathetic, did not quite understand my feisty reaction to the situation.

Neither did my minister husband. Twenty-three years later, I still remember how I seethed when he gently suggested that my issues with mortality were the real cause of my anger, not the idea that I would never have another child. I was in no frame of mind to have him tell me what I was feeling. I said I needed him to be my husband, not my minister.

I hadn't gotten the answers I needed at home, or from the surgeon who was known for his outstanding skills but ranked zero on bedside manner. I wanted to be heard and supported because this surgery meant a huge loss for me. I had always thought I would have a large family. I had to redefine that three was a family, as opposed to the six that was my birth family. So I called my friend Terri, a therapist. When I told her I was having trouble letting go of my uterus, she said, "Meet me in my office tomorrow at eight o'clock." I felt better already.

Terri listened to me in a way that no one else had as I dealt with the overwhelming reality that my daughter would never have a sibling. As I shared my guilt for having had two abortions prior to marrying my husband, and the unhappy circumstances surrounding those decisions, Terri counseled me to remember the courage it had taken when my back was against the wall, and to focus on that rather than the guilt. Terri encouraged me to share my experiences with my daughter when she got older. That seemed reasonable but frightening. Like Scarlett O'Hara, I thought, I will think about that tomorrow. I felt much better when I left Terri's office.

The day I arrived at the hospital, I was functioning pretty well until I was given one of the last papers to sign that said, in effect, "As a result of this procedure, you will be sterile." The escalating emotions at the absolute impossibility of birthing another child, along with the recently buried feeling of help-lessness, shattered my composure. My tears turned to sobs, dissolving my self-control right in front of the admitting person, my daughter, and my husband.

I ran out of the office, through the waiting room, and made a turn away from the open lounge where families waited near massive, closed doors marked "No ADMITTANCE." On my right were elevators to the hospital rooms, not a good choice. Farther along was the cafeteria, also not an option. My only alterna-tive was the door on my left, marked "CHAPEL." I hurried in, sat down, and wept. It felt good to grieve for the children I wouldn't have. My responsible self knew that at some point I had to surrender, but for now, in this empty, dark, womb-like room, I let my sorrow flow.

My daughter and husband had scampered after me and now stood before me, dumbfounded. My daughter looked deeply concerned and sad. My husband appeared frightened. When the flood of tears subsided, I said, "I'm sorry." Which was untrue. But my good-girl script was strong, and I felt that I should apologize. And now they were soothing me. My daughter even asked me if I wanted to go home. *What a gal*, I thought. *She's more empathetic than my husband.*

That night, I was alone in the hospital after visiting hours. I went downstairs to the chapel and asked the Great One for courage, strength, and guidance. When I got back to my room, there was a familiar figure sitting in the chair waiting for me, even though it was after visiting hours. Nancy was my spiritual sister, and we'd lived in the same town four years earlier. She was an aging hippy who had graduated with honors from the school of hard knocks. Nancy sat with me and guided me through a meditation in which I visualized myself waltzing in my favorite meadow of wildflowers in dazzling Technicolor. She did a laying on of hands that was supposed to distribute my energy where I most needed it. As I closed my eyes to sleep, Nancy kissed my forehead, or maybe it was my third eye, and bid me good-night.

Early the next morning, the nurse who got me ready for the surgery said in a kindly, thoughtful, almost reverential voice, "Honey, you look so peaceful. You have a glow about your face and head." We stared at each other with no need for explanations.

At five thirty, I had been transferred to a gurney and was about to be wheeled out of the hospital room down the hall to the elevator marked, "NO ADMITTANCE." At that moment of no return, my daughter appeared, followed by her dad. The night before she had asked him to drive her to the hospital so she could see me before the operation. And when he tried to talk her out of it, saying that the staff probably wouldn't let them in, it was against hospital policy, and they might be too late to see me, she countered by saying she'd get a friend's mother to take her. Apparently, that shamed him into driving her. She had told him, "Dad, Mom needs me."

Lying on the gurney, traveling down the hall with my daughter holding my hand and bending down close to my face, I gave up the battle with sweet assurance that I was victorious. I had my daughter, and she was all the children I needed.

Leap of Faith

I was forty-three years old, wearing my academic cap and gown. The first person I committed to was myself. I had attended fifteen of these graduations. But this time, sitting under the hot June sun that day in 1984, I was seeing the future.

An elderly woman onstage was being honored for her umpteen years of teaching nursing at this community college. The president was elaborating on her virtues, as well as the college's gratitude for her knowledge and sacrifice as a model instructor and dedicated member of the college community.

I had an instant snapshot of myself in twenty-five years, wrinkled and resentful for how I had spent my working life. I said to myself, "If you don't make a decision to change, then that will be you. Except for the wrinkles, that *is* you."

That *aha!* moment began my journey to quitting dental hygiene teaching and becoming a sociologist. This was no small leap of faith. I had taken one sociology course in junior college in 1960. Was I crazy to think I could do this? I told my inner critic to shut up and proceeded with enough energy to fuel a jet plane.

I told no one for a time. In between working, mothering a middle-school daughter, and being married, which included filling the role of "minister's wife," I began investigating universities. It was my intention to go to a top public university within a reasonable geographical area, and to enter as a full-time day student. I wanted to be part of a scholarly field doing research that focused on human conditions and social problems.

A huge part of my staying with a job that was no longer fulfilling had to do with economic security. I also worried that my career change might negatively affect my daughter's choice of college. Both my husband and I had put ourselves through university, and we wanted to give our daughter the gift of attending the college of her choice without economic influence and studying without money worries.

For me, 1984 was a year of many losses. I lost my uterus and with it any dream that I might have another child. When I resigned from my job, I also lost my husband's emotional support and understanding. He hadn't been supportive of the hysterectomy either, suggesting that my emotional response to it stemmed from my fear of death. And regarding my job, he evoked the idea that the second half of one's life was an internal journey, and the outer one of success was, by implication, for the less spiritually evolved. I was not buying his ideas.

Prior to my surgery, I had met with a therapist friend who helped me realize that I needed time to grieve my losses from my miscarriages and abortions, as well as the mother and husband I could not depend on for emotional support. In all fairness, my husband did give me financial security. I needed to forgive them and myself. I was convinced that the way forward was graduate school and my time was now.

In my pursuit of applying to two universities, I met with faculty to discuss my application. One woman professor advised me, "Bury the fact that you're a dental hygienist. There is a stereotype that would be difficult to overcome." I was grateful for her honesty.

In addition to my dental hygiene teaching, I applied for a part-time research assistant position at my first-choice university to improve my application. I got the job, and I loved it. I was intellectually challenged doing research with people who were curious and eager to explore ideas. It was everything I did not have at my teaching job. I was engaged in research that I believed was contributing to the understanding of issues for people living with HIV/AIDS. Barbara, the principal investigator, supported my application to graduate school and treated me with respect. She encouraged me as I learned on the job, as did three other members of the team. It was not unusual to receive handwritten notes of encouragement. At times we worked with no thought of the clock. Barbara gave me the opportunity to present her research at a national meeting in Washington, DC. She was an exceptional mentor.

My daughter, Monica, was overwhelmingly supportive of me and my plan during this time. She was so confident of my success that she presented me with a handmade gift, wrapped in red tissue paper. Opening the gift, I was stunned to see a tiny rectangular pillow with "DR. BARNES" cross-stitched in primary colors, each letter outlined in an opposing color. Tears filled my eyes, as I feared I did not deserve this recognition and had doubts that I would earn this distinction. This treasure still sits on the desk in my study.

My husband, meanwhile, was in a crisis in his ministry at the church where he was serving. The congregation had failed, by a very narrow margin, to call the first openly gay male as associate minister. Ken confessed he wanted to quit. But a wise person in the church counseled him that there were other people who were quitting, or wanting to quit, and he should consider that in his decision.

One evening as Ken and I were sitting in the sauna, he floated the idea that he might want to take a sabbatical. He proposed that the three of us go, perhaps to Boston, where Monica could start high school and find a dance studio to support her growing passion. And hopefully I could find some teaching work.

"I don't think it's a good idea to take Monica away at the start of high school," I said. "To take her away from her friends that she has had since first grade seems unfair."

"That may be true," he said, "but I think you are being too protective."

"I expect to start my doctoral program this fall, so I don't want to move," I told him.

Ken's response was a look that conveyed his doubts about my hopes and plans.

I said, "Why don't you take this opportunity to do whatever it is that you want to do, without trying to accommodate Monica and me. You should think about your needs and what would rejuvenate you."

Ken seemed relieved, but still uncertain.

"Of course, I can't speak for Monica," I said. "You'll need to talk with her about it."

Some weeks later, I heard from my second-choice university, which denied me admission. I had confidence, or perhaps it was strong hope, that my first choice would come through. However, in June 1987, I received a letter from them denying admission. I was ashamed of myself for dreaming so large. Though I was sad and disappointed, I knew I would reapply, so I called the university and made an appointment.

"How can I improve my application for next year?" I asked the faculty member. He offered a generic reply about improving my GRE score and publishing more. He seemed bored and eager to get me out of his office.

"Is there a wait list?" I asked as I was leaving.

He said there was not.

The next day at work, the research team took me out to a popular pizza place for dinner. They tried with great enthusiasm to convince me why a doctorate was not that important and why I did not want one, pointing out how I had escaped years of educational punishment. I wasn't convinced but appreciated their efforts. Victor even shared how he had not gotten into Harvard initially but had been on their wait list and was later admitted.

When the bill came, Barbara insisted on paying. She handed over a check to the waitress, who said, "We don't take checks." But after the waitress examined it, she looked pleased and said, "Well, since you have a PhD, we can accept it." This negated every argument the group had proposed to me, and we had a fine laugh. I was trying to be a good sport, despite my feelings of rejection.

Taking off for our family's Fourth of July vacation, I was determined not to give up hope. I would retake the GRE, and I would work on publications with the research team. However, once at the Lake House, a family property on the Barnes side, I was not in the mood to think about that. I spent hours swimming, reading novels, recovering from my two years of admission preparations, and regretting my increasingly disappointing work teaching dental hygiene.

Returning home feeling refreshed, I found a week-old message on our answering machine: "Please call as soon as possible." As I was dialing, I hoped Susan, the administrative assistant at UC San Francisco, was still in the office.

She said, "If you are available, we would like to offer you admission to the program for fall 1987."

"Yes, of course," I replied.

In retrospect, I hope I remembered to say, "Thank you."

The rest of that summer was a whirlwind. My husband left in June for his six-month sabbatical, my daughter went to dance camp, and I read sociology theory. My husband had finalized his sabbatical plans to enter a monastery in Montreal for five months as the lone Protestant minister among the Catholic brothers. Ken boarded a Greyhound bus in Richmond, California. He planned to take a month-long trip across the country, stopping overnight to experience small-town America. He promised to call every Sunday.

As the months passed, Monica and I enjoyed a new lifestyle. We ate what and when we wanted and went to bed when we were sleepy, with no need to accommodate early dinners and bedtimes, or quiet time on Saturday nights. She had her friends over for pizza and movies. We enjoyed skipping Sunday services and feeling guilt-free.

In the fall, she entered high school, and I began the first of five years of study. We both studied hard, sometimes together at night in the university law library. We invited her study groups to the house, and I enjoyed cooking spaghetti dinners for their hungry minds and stomachs.

When Ken returned the week of Thanksgiving, we three had some adjusting to do. We had all been influenced by our new experiences. How were we to reconfigure our lifestyle to accommodate our family and individual needs? Ken offered to do more household chores and took on washing his own laundry after he got tired of complaining about not having clean folded socks in his drawer. He eventually did the weekly shopping too. I appreciated his gestures and his willingness to be part of a family where each of us had duties in the home and responsibilities in the world. It was hard to deal with the tensions and difficult to watch all of us adjust, but particularly Ken, who struggled to find his place in the ever-changing family dynamics of a teenage daughter with her first boyfriend and her graduate school mother who had resigned from being a minister's wife.

On Christmas morning, our daughter gave us an unexpected gift to help to ease our relationship during this time. It was a record of a song I didn't know called "Old Friend."

"Old Friend, it's so nice to feel you hold me again, welcome back into my life again. Old friend, this is where our happy ending begins."

Graduate school was challenging, intellectually stimulating, and exhausting. It became painful to recognize my lack of essay writing skills since I had been limited to taking notes in dental charts for so many years. At times I felt like I was in second grade, being punished by having my grammar corrected with red pencil. When it came to theory, I was at a distinct disadvantage from my cohorts. It was a challenge to figure out what Karl Marx was ultimately saying as I read through pages of how silkworms work, and what was pivotal about Max Weber's writings on bureaucracy. My fellow students had come with knowledge that I did not have, which left me playing catch-up and hiring a tutor. My second year got better after I proposed my research, received funding, joined a writing group, and was mentored through my dissertation by an internationally known sociologist. I made three lifelong friends and graduated on track in 1992, the year my daughter completed her freshman year of college. My husband flew to meet her and help her drive home in time for my graduation.

The joy of completing my dream career as a sociologist was overshadowed by the fact that I was still teaching dental hygiene. At the same time, I had begun teaching courses at two other colleges, attempting to get my foot in the door for a teaching contract with benefits. My graduate school buddy called me a "Roads Scholar." I was teaching an eight o'clock class, driving across town to teach dental hygiene from eleven to four, and then motoring twenty-two miles east for a four o'clock class.

Three years after graduation, I was making progress toward a contract position at the state university and starting my own research with funding. I was still teaching dental hygiene, but I chose not to share that part of my life as I presented myself as a sociologist.

At that time, I had been accepted for a three-week residency at Hedgebrook, a fully funded creative writing program. One afternoon, I took off with Victoria, a fellow writer, to drive to Friday Harbor in Washington State. On the ferry, she asked me what I did for work. I told her about all my jobs, including teaching dental hygiene, and how much I hated it. She burst out laughing. She had known me for two and half weeks, had read my creative writing, and could not believe what I had just told her. It was a relief not to hide that part of myself as I had been doing since entering graduate school.

"Why do you do that when you should be writing?" she asked.

When I returned from my residency, I wrote my letter of resignation to escape the job I'd committed to leaving so long ago, freeing myself to teach sociology and do research full-time. I broke out of the cocoon of job and financial security, allowing myself to reach for a new reality and to become the butterfly I longed to be.

I Missed Mom

I regret that I attended Virginia Oleson's Medical Sociology class that day in 1989, the spring of my second year in the doctoral program at UC San Francisco, instead of going home to be with my father and siblings the day after Mom died. My class assignment was to present an analysis of Friedman's typology on the "sick role" and engage my fellow students in what I hoped would be a lively discussion. Wading through his research, I had taken notes, typed out key points, and applied my emerging sociological critical thinking skills. In preparation, I made sure I was aware of current terminology so as to appear "cutting edge." I had worked hard, and I was prepared.

Dr. Oleson, an icon in this field of study, allowed us to call her "Ginny," though I had some hesitation every time I did. At home we referred to her as my second-grade teacher because of how thoroughly she marked up my essays in red pencil for errors in spelling, grammar, and, at times, logic. She was a stickler for use of commas and precise about two spaces between the author and the date in a reference list. I felt I had a lot to learn from her, which might give you an idea of how insecure I felt in her course. I wanted and needed to impress Ginny.

When I called Ginny to tell her my mom had died the night before I was to give my assignment, I would not entertain her suggestion of postponing. In what I thought of as my busy life, I did not see how I was going to reschedule my class assignment with just a few weeks left in the quarter. So why did I bother to tell her? Was I expecting sympathy? Was I hoping for leniency in grading?

Though I was raised with the value that family comes first, I did not go to be with my dad on the day Mom died, as my three siblings had done. I stayed home that night. Neither Dad nor my siblings commented on my decision. If they had an opinion, they never verbalized it to me. I suppose another expectation I inherited was the importance of fulfilling work responsibilities.

The next day, after teaching in the morning, I drove to San Francisco to present my assignment in the afternoon class before leaving for my childhood home in Napa, about an hour away.

My mom's death was a relief to our entire family. "It was a blessing," is what we all said. Mom had had early-onset dementia, which I suppose distinguished it from late-onset dementia. The science of memory loss was still being discovered. She was seventy-six when she died, and she'd spent her last four years in a nursing home, where she was progressively unable to walk, feed herself, or communicate. In every way she was not herself. She went from knowing me, to recognizing that I was one of her daughters, to calling me her mother, to not responding to me at all. She only recognized my dad, who visited her twice daily to feed and comfort her. As Uncle Roy said of my father, "Romi earned a place in heaven."

It was my first close personal experience with death, except for my grandparents. My maternal grandmother died a month before I gave birth to my daughter in 1973. My mom had protected me from the initial news of Nana's death by first telling my husband, who gently relayed the message to me. Mom was concerned I would miscarry, an experience I'd had with two previous pregnancies.

When my paternal grandfather died a week after I graduated from high school in 1958, I was only seventeen years old, and then too I'd been protected by my parents from the experience and details of death, except to attend his open-casket funeral.

I seldom saw my maternal grandfather, as Nana had divorced when my mom was six or seven. We rarely visited him, and, as far as I recall, he never visited us. I have few memories of him, and little recollection of his funeral.

Looking back, I realize I failed myself in not going home that day. I regret not having stayed in my childhood home in Napa to be with my dad and siblings after my mom's death. Instead, I chose to give a paper. I justified my decision by telling myself that working three-quarter time and being a full-time doctoral student, mother, and wife left little room for adjustments to life or, in this case, death.

I came to realize how cheaply I had sold myself. I completed my assignment, but I paid a high price for not being with Dad and my siblings. I missed out on the sharing of those initial raw emotions about Mom's death. Eventually, I came to learn that it resulted in a prolonged mourning as well. It cost me the missed hours we might have spent together: those hours of taking care of each other, of just spending time in Mom's home.

I missed so many things about Mom: sitting on her bed, admiring the crochet bedspread that her hands had made. I missed sharing the view out of Mom and Dad's bedroom window of our football field-sized backyard where Dad had taught us hopscotch as soon as we could walk, and later how to ride a pogo stick he made for us. Seasonally we played football, basketball, and baseball. Our childhood bedroom that I once shared with my sisters had the same view, but not Mom's beloved, old-fashioned blue hydrangeas that became my favorite flower. I missed how she was such a good speller but encouraged us to use the dictionary. I missed that she read *Alice in Wonderland* to me, and took us to the library every week, and that she was a Book-of-the-Month Club reader. I missed, as a child, admiring her delicate blue glass Evening in Paris perfume bottle with a gold tassel at the neck. I missed the smell of Mom as she dressed for a pretend evening in Paris, when she and Dad would go dancing at St. John's Church's social hall, sponsored by the Italian Catholic Federation Club. It was a regular event among the hours, days, and years of pushing the vacuum, mopping the floors, cleaning the toilet, the stove, the kids, and the dog—a respite from the dirty work.

I missed Mom.

1993: My Destiny Year

I am not a religious person, but this story begins at a sacred retreat. It was Sunday, July 18, 1993, when I left my home and endured stop-and-go traffic through the Bay Area until it and the fog cleared past San Jose. I welcomed the warmth of the sun and the open fields of artichokes and strawberries as I drove through the Central Valley food basket glancing at the passing roadside stands at Gilroy and Salinas on Highway 101. The mental prelude for leaving behind my frenzied life, if not my concerns, began in preparation for the retreat. It wasn't until I came to San Luis Obispo, three hours into the five-hour long drive with what remained of the 343-mile drive along the coastline of California, that I felt like I could take a deep breath. The smell of the concentrated summer sea, full of the promise of fun, filled my white Volvo with all four windows down. The company of the sounds of the ocean floating into my car was a welcome replacement for the NPR radio station I'd left behind and out of transmission range in Salinas.

I was retreating from an overstuffed lifestyle of managing the responsibilities of wife, mother, and a new career. My husband was still waiting for me to return to the more traditional duties I'd left behind when I'd gone to graduate school at age forty-six. My daughter had completed her first year of college. I was currently directing three research projects, and I'd taught six new courses at three different colleges within a fifty-mile radius of my home during the past year, my inauguration year as a newly minted PhD sociologist at age fifty-two.

I was feeling free and generous of spirit as I pulled into La Casa de Maria, on land originally inhabited by the Chumash people then colonized by Spain. In 1780, King Charles IV had granted this area to the Franciscan missions. In the late 1880s, it was sold to a rancher who planted citrus orchards. In the 1920s, new owners built an elaborate estate in the Spanish Revival style that was completed in the 1930s. When it went on the market in the 1940s, it was purchased by the Sisters of the Immaculate Heart of Los Angeles as housing for novitiates. In 1974, the community started the Center for Spiritual Renewal, which was at that time housed in the former mansion just south of Santa Barbara in Montecito.

It had been a year since I'd completed my doctorate, and I'd said "yes" to too many projects and courses in search of my niche. I was a baby sociologist, developing a new career and struggling to shed a twenty-four-year tenure position as a dental hygiene teacher in a community college. When I arrived at La Casa de Maria, I was feeling overwhelmed.

I had come to the retreat to be in the presence of Ursula, a former nun and mother superior turned wife and family counselor, who was married to a former university president turned play-wright and living in subsidized housing for artists in New York City. This alone was enough for me to like her. Also, I had been on several weekend retreats under Ursula's guidance, initially at the encouragement of my friend Ruth. However, this commitment was more intensive, as the retreat would last one week.

I was not sure I could "retreat" for that length of time, so I had hauled a cardboard file box full of Xerox copies of about forty journal articles and five books to review, along with my 150-page qualifying exam for the purpose of submitting a condensed version for academic publication. The article was to be a critical review of the literature of just about everything anyone had ever said on my dissertation topic, "Disclosure." Disclosure is about revealing, exposing, leaking, confessing, sharing secret information about oneself, or being discovered by others who gain knowledge of your secret by deduction or guesswork. I had long been interested in the process of sharing and withholding secrets, under what circumstances, and the resulting consequences. Troy Duster, a well-known sociologist, has said, "Scratch a theory, find a biography."

This Ursula-led retreat was a spiritual one based in the religious foundation of Catholicism and attended primarily by Catholics in good standing. I was not one of them, though I had been raised Catholic. In college I had questioned the church's doctrines on divorce, abortion, and homosexuality. Then, in my late twenties, I had married a Protestant minister.

The retreat was exclusively for women by design and dealt with taking care of oneself spiritually. The title was "Women Connecting—Sharing Strengths, Taking Risks, Making Changes." I signed up for the retreat because of Ursula's leadership, not because of its title, though in retrospect I found it serendipitous.

The format consisted of morning and evening sessions with Ursula presenting ideas along with personal writing exercises and small group sharing. There was very little mention of biblical text. The afternoons were for reflection, study of available materials, spiritual direction by appointment with Ursula, and relaxation, including swimming. There was a masseuse on site. I indulged. Mass was said on Saturday night. I passed.

During the week, I spent many hours in the tepid, unheated swimming pool; at the beach with its huge swing that took me out over the ocean; and in an outdoor "office" I made, a haven on a secluded bench in a thicket of eucalyptus trees. Let me assure you, however, that I never missed a session with Ursula, including an intense, supportive, and humorous one-on-one meeting.

At the appointed time, I met Ursula in a small, cozy room, formerly the gardener's house, with high windows open to the woods. As we sat facing one another in comfortable and worn upholstered club chairs I thought, *I have never met anyone one in whom kindness, wisdom, and perception combine in such a way as they do in Ursula.*

I had always admired her beauty, with her short hair curled close to her fair, smooth skin, the stylish way she walked and dressed, always in pastel colors with matching jewelry. She expressed herself elegantly, using her age-spotted hands with manicured nails as she spoke. Her compassionate eyes drew me in, releasing any tension or anxiety that had accompanied me through the door.

As Ursula leaned closer and looked at me, she saw sadness despite my enthusiastic, lively persona. I wear sadness as a veil around my eyes at times. And while at times my eyes are a beacon of brightness, most people can't discern the difference between my moods. I often don't even acknowledge it myself.

On this day in July, Ursula saw the sadness. She said when she saw me on the first day of the retreat, her first thought had been that I looked sad and serious. Seriousness was a path I had chosen, but I hated to acknowledge the sadness. I confessed to Ursula in that moment that I had come to progressively realize that my spouse did not find my jokes funny, nor did he understand my sense of humor. He thought I laughed too loudly and talked about myself too much. Ursula understood that my married life, due to my husband's ministry, had been involved with death, sickness, and trouble. I shared that, since graduate school, I had chosen a research focus that was fraught with issues of betrayal, discrimination, sexism, racism, illness, and death. Ursula said, "Of course. I appreciate that about your work, and I thank you for it as well." I felt enclosed in her deep wisdom.

Ursula suggested it was time to play. Had I been so focused on making a new career that I'd forgotten how to have fun? Ursula counseled me to do activities that freed me—she suggested painting and dancing, but as a child would do—not to do the best painting or dancing, but just to fool around. She also suggested gathering photos of myself as a child and enlarging a few for my study to remind me of what joy I had shown as a child. I would take her suggestions on the photos immediately upon returning home. As a result of Ursula's prompting, I began a lifelong hobby of water color painting that started in Boston the following summer where I purchased a Winsor & Newton travel container of twelve tubes of paint. As Sir Winston Churchill said, "Just to paint is great fun. . . . Try it if you have not done so before you die." But more poignant was the mutual friendship with Ursula that continued to be a cornerstone in my life until she passed at age 91 in March 2014.

Toward the end of the retreat, Ursula asked us to do an exercise on the question: "What is your destiny?" I wasn't enthused. But I had such respect and admiration for Ursula that I gave it my best shot.

I took off in pursuit of an outdoor nook and attempted to quiet myself. I would describe myself as a morning, afternoon, and late evening type person who wakes up and is raring to go. In a retreat setting, I'm conscious to monitor my enthusiasm to become more introspective. I sat on a bench dedicated "To Our Friend, Brick," shaded by a mature oak tree under the July morning sun. It was quiet except for the birds whistling in a variety of dialects. The scene began to calm down my body, but not my mind, as I wondered whether the assortment of birds could understand each other's language. Good question, but beyond my comprehension at the moment. If I listened carefully and patiently, I could hear the ocean over the distant hum of traffic on Highway 1. It felt delicious outside with the fresh air, slight breeze, and warmth, in contrast with the cool, stale indoor air. This was a good place to exhale and remind myself to breathe.

"What is your destiny?" It seemed a powerful concept, but I don't believe in predestination. I believe in free will and hard work. My brainy self informed me that we know ourselves primarily in interaction with others and in how we observe ourselves reflected by the way people perceive us, or how we understand they perceive us.

"*Halt*!" a loud feminine voice exclaimed from nowhere. "Please," it added very quietly. As I was thinking my way around the idea of destiny, it turned up, not in a vision, but in a voice. This was not a burning bush experience, nor a road to Damascus encounter where your sight is temporarily taken and your name is stolen; not a dream, or a visitation like the angel descending upon the Virgin Mary. It was a comfortable, absolute, and quiet "yes" experience, like taking a walk in the very early morning when the possibility of peace seems promising. Destiny told me, "You are to tell women's stories."

Telling women's stories, hmmm. What an idea. I knew what I'd heard to be true, as I knew my eyes are brown without looking in the mirror. I liked my destiny, but I wasn't educationally prepared for this. Telling women's stories, to me, seemed to assume creative writing skills. I didn't know how I would do it. At the beginning of a new career, I was still just a burgeoning sociologist, with an idea of preparing my manuscript for publication. I had primarily interviewed men and only a few women.

Besides, as a floundering academic writer, it was hard enough to get scientific journals interested in women's issues, aside from a few feminist publications that every social scientist of similar bent was competing for. Taking on the task of a successful writer of narrative nonfiction was daunting. But that practical consideration aside, it felt good to know my destiny: I was to tell women's stories. After the anxiety of "I'm not prepared for this," I felt calm and even serene.

It was the next to the last lunch of the six-day retreat, and like any intense gathering of people toward the end, there was a gushing of emotions, genuine but very powerful, from some who had never previously shared a thought in a group gathering. For me there was a sense of guilt, the gift that keeps on giving, about not extending myself more and regret for some emotional connections I might have missed.

In this newly opened, vulnerable state, I found myself seated next to Valerie. Valerie did serious work as a social worker but with the joy of a comedian. As this was one of our last meals together, some of our conversation traveled to what we did "back home." It turned out that we shared a work life that included women's health, HIV/AIDS, and social issues. I was impressed by her joy, her serious work, her sense of humor, and her profound interest in helping people. It turned out that she was a lay member of the Immaculate Heart Community that had sponsored this retreat.

As we talked, I shared how powerful the destiny exercise had been for me and how I'd learned I was to tell women's stories. I told her about that "Halt!" voice and how it was loud and clear. Valerie stared at me for a moment without speaking. Then she said, "I know a woman I think you should meet."

I was floored by the synchronicity of what she proceeded to share with me. Choosing to sit next to this relative stranger was no coincidence. I figured my destiny experience was a gift from God. And sitting next to Valerie was divine intervention. The long and short of it was that she wanted me to meet and interview Meria, a young woman with HIV, and Valerie was willing to arrange for it to happen before I started my drive back home the next day. We were both enthusiastic and agreed to work out the details.

In preparation, I called my husband to have him go into my study and find and fax me some of my research material, including the informed consent details necessary for human subject research.

Being selected by Valerie to interview this woman thrilled me. I knew from experience how difficult it was to locate and recruit women for research about their HIV experiences, because of the enormous stigma for women with HIV. Culturally, women's roles were to be mothers and protectors of children. But frequently, within multiple social institutions, such as family, church, and employment, women with HIV were seen as vectors of the virus, even though statistically, the most frequent mode of transmission for women was being infected by HIV-positive men who injected drugs.

The next morning, July 23, 1993, over breakfast, Valerie gave me handwritten directions with a map to Meria's home. I was to meet her at one o'clock that afternoon. I was ready and eager to proceed. I knew how to do this. I had interviewed people with HIV, mostly men and a few women for my dissertation. Fortunately, I had brought a cassette player to listen to my music, but unfortunately, I had no blank tapes. I looked over my music collection and chose "Baroque Music, Super Learning," a tape I had listened to while studying classic theories of Marx, Weber, and Durkheim in the hopes of being able to remember them. I had no regrets in taping over it for Meria's interview.

Two days after my destiny was made known to me, I met Meria in the most unlikely and alienating part of California, revealing the cumulative depleting effects of years of trickledown Reaganomics, despite the Silicon Valley boon. After a few hours' drive, I was facing Meria and pressing "RECORD." I embraced my destiny and thus began my journey as a creative writer. Ursula and her retreat gave me all that was promised in the title: "Women Connecting—Sharing Strengths, Taking

Risks, Making Changes." Because of it all, I was ready to make changes in my prescribed role of sociologist. Because of the "Halt!" experience, I was eager to add the role of creative writer. The identity still feels like it belongs to someone else. No. That is my inner critic in her most negative mood. And that is a voice I am not listening to.

Meria, May You
Rest in Peace

"I don't think I will rest in peace. I will not go in peace
until I have completed the arrangements for my son,
Johnny. Tony's left it all up to me."

—MERIA, JULY 23, 1993

Meria began telling me her story:

My husband, Tony, called me from the hospital where
he had been for the past few days for tests. He had been
tired all the time. You know, he slept all the time. He
got up, went to work, came home, took a shower, and
he was out. There would be a lot of arguments. You
know, I'd say, "You never want to do anything. You're
always tired. You're always sleepy. You're young, you
shouldn't be like that." We just never ever thought—
even when we were going through all the tests, it never
ever went through our minds, you know, is it this? You
know, we didn't know none of the symptoms.

I recognized the symptoms as soon as her twenty-eight-year-old husband, Tony, opened the door. I had driven from early morning to their home on a summer day known weather-wise as a real scorcher. And in this dry, dusty, rural town, the heat was intensified. You know you're in the country when there are no sidewalks, no stoplights, and the kids, dogs, and cats share the road without visible boundaries. I drove my white Volvo with extra caution.

I had never been to this town before. Had no reason. It was not near a university or on the usual vacation trail. It was part of the vast Central Valley of California. Even if you drove from San Francisco to Los Angeles, you would have to go way out of your way to go through this town. I knew I looked out of place.

Meria was not expecting me for an hour, so I had time for lunch. As I drove around, I realized my choices were limited. At a Mexican lunch counter in a shopping center, I ordered and sat at one of the two tables. My presence seemed to have a quieting effect on the conversations. I ate and left having spoken only a few words: "One chicken enchilada, no beans or rice, and a Coke, please." I was conscious that my speech made me stand out among the male laborers.

Tony and Meria's home was in a tract where the houses looked alike except that some had more stuff in the yard than others. There were few trees, no shade, no green lawns, and no flowerbeds. Directly across the street was a large lot loaded with old buses and trailers surrounded by a cyclone wire fence. Walking from the car to the front door, I began to perspire, and the hot, dusty wind powdered the sweat to my skin.

Tony answered the door in his pajamas, thin flannel, long-sleeved ones that seemed out of place in this heat. He acknowledged me with a "Hello" but did not meet my eyes. He backed away in a low bow, speaking no words in response to my introduction. He didn't return to an erect position, but turned and shuffled, like a very old man, as he led me to Meria.

We passed through a gloomy, crowded living room where all the shades were drawn. It reminded me of Mom's system of beating the heat, but I thought now, as I did as a kid, that the room might be cooler, but the lack of sun took the life out of it. We continued down a short hall to the bedroom. I observed Tony as he returned to the living room sofa where he had been watching television. He was very thin, with grayish-pale skin, obviously ill. Disease was draining the life out of this young man. I wanted to thank him for opening the door for me, for escorting me to Meria, but more than that, I wanted to apologize for causing him exertion, for intruding into his home, for the illness. But I said nothing.

Meria, by contrast, was full of life. As I entered the bedroom, she was busy finishing up a phone call. She was instructing the doctor or nurse on the line as to what medication she needed, how much, and when. She was in control in a pleasant but insistent way, and I took a few moments to observe her.

She was propped up in bed on top of the covers, fully dressed. Her long, dark brown, curly hair framed her explicitly beautiful face. Her dark features, wide mouth, and large, decisive eyes reflected her classic mixed Mexican and Cuban heritage. Her makeup was apparent but not overdone. She wore a white, short-sleeved blouse with elastic at the cuffs and neckline. The large ruffles on the scooped neckline and sleeves accentuated her full bosom and youthful figure. She wore red shorts and had bare feet. Meria did not look sick. The only evidence of illness was the almost-hidden catheter in her chest, which was at times exposed by the ruffles when she moved. It seemed obvious that her dress had been chosen to accommodate her pride and her catheter.

The well-lit bedroom had an orderliness about it, despite being crowded. The bed took up almost the entire room, jutting up against the long sideboard whose sole function appeared to be to hold the oversized television set, which was on but without sound. There was a nightstand with the latest high-tech telephone and a lamp. There was no place to sit down. Meria motioned for me to sit on the bed. I did so with some hesitation, but there was no other choice, not even floor space.

Of all the interviews I've done for my research on disclosure with women with HIV/AIDS over the years, this is the only one I've conducted in a home. My usual style was to meet interviewees at the place they went to for medical or social services. I knew this interview was going to be different, but I was not prepared for the surprises that followed or that the haunting story would be housed within me, waiting to be released years later.

Meria greeted me with a bright, cheerful smile. She spoke quickly, looking me directly in the eye, and expressed interest in the interview process. She did not defer to me, nor was she in awe of research. She had a story, and she wanted to tell it. I had come highly recommended by two people she trusted. It was not hard to put her at ease; I imagined she thought the same of me.

She was eager to start telling her story. I had to slow her down to do the preliminary informed consent and discuss her rights as a research participant. She listened and waited until I finished. She had no questions. However, she instructed me to spell her name correctly, Meria with an "e," not the usual "a." She was funny about this. Precision about her name was essential and not to be left to chance. I made a note, and Meria continued her story:

> *When we first got married, Tony was always tired. But it had increased, you know, the tiredness was just getting worse. He was tired, but he would say, "Okay, let's go, we're going to either go out to dinner or a*

dance or I'll take you out here." Any little thing, you know? I felt that he was so young, why does he always want to be sleeping? And when we went to visit any relatives or whatever, as soon as we got there, he just sat on the couch and fell asleep. And that used to upset me, and I would say, "You know, we come to visit, and you fall asleep." I just couldn't understand.

Tony went to the clinic just to have a physical and maybe get some vitamins or something to increase his energy because we were getting ready to go on vacation. We were going to be camping for a week, and then we would come back and maybe drive down south to visit his sister for three or four days before we came back home. But he says, "I have some sort of flu or something and I haven't taken care of it."

At first, they thought it was some sort of cancer. I don't know. His father is his stepfather so, you know? We had just recently lost his grandfather, but biologically they're nothing to him, so there was no connection like saying, "Well it runs in the family." We don't know from his dad's side of the family, his real father's side of the family. He's never met him. We haven't been able to find him. We tried to find him at the time to see what history, maybe it ran in the family. On his mom's side of the family as far as we knew, there's no cancer.

It led to where the nurse said, "Well, okay, let me run some blood work. The nurse ran the test, and she came into the room, and she was just like—her face— she looked shocked. She said, "I'm not going to try to worry you, I don't want you to go off the hammer here, but you're walking around with no immune system. Your white count is extremely low and so is your red count. There is no explanation from what you have told me. I really don't know."

So then the doctor came in, she was a doctor, so she had got another doctor and they talked, and he came in and he says, "I want you to go. . . ." I mean he goes, "I need to get you—hospitalize you, you need some blood," and he says, "and we need to increase your white count and your red count."

So Tony was in the hospital for six days. About three days into the week, they had run all the tests that they could think of, and everything was negative. So finally the doctor came in and says, "Well everything's negative. The only test I have not asked you if we could do is the HIV/AIDS test." And Tony's like, "Oh, that's no problem." He goes, "I know for sure I don't have that." They took it, and about four days later we got the results back. When Tony called, I was home with the baby, our son, Johnny. He was about three-and-a-half months old. I was already very paranoid about the baby, very, you know, any little sneeze, cough, I mean I would just go off, you know, run to the doctor or run to the emergency room. I was just terrified. I thought that he was not going to live past four months old, since the first one had died at four months. I just—there was something in me that just, that, I was, I guess I was kind of overprotective. Any little thing I would . . . My mom's like, "Calm down. Don't do that to him. You know he's going to be fine. You have to think positive, you can't think negative." She's on and on and on. I was like, okay.

"I need you to come right now," Tony insisted over the phone.

"What's wrong? Can't you tell me on the phone?" I said. I was always worried about taking the baby out right after a bath.

"I can't tell you over the phone, get over here right now." And he hung up.

*So I get the baby, I get in the car, and I drop him
off at my aunt's house. I told my aunt, "I got to go to
the hospital. I don't know what's wrong; Tony didn't
want to tell me. He doesn't sound sick." It just didn't,
it didn't click in my mind saying, ooh, and maybe he
got the results back—I didn't think of that.*

*My husband's first words when he was told that
his AIDS test was positive, when he got me and sat
me down and knelt down, and he was trying to say
something to me, and he was just like, you know, he
couldn't believe it. And I was like, "Well what? I just
never ever thought of it. When he said, "I—my test
came back positive." Um, I remember saying, "Do you
want to run by me, slowly tell me this again. You are
joking, right?"*

He said, "No."

*I said, "Okay, well, I guess we can handle it.
There's nothing much we can do." I go, "We have to
be strong. Let's get some literature on this. Let's get
to know it."*

*There was just no way my husband could have
AIDS. Because he was not gay, you know, and he'd
never used drugs. I guess Tony got AIDS with somebody
he dated when he was in the Navy. I don't know much
about it because I'd rather not know much about it.*

*I do confess I have always been a very jealous
girlfriend and wife. I didn't want to know that my
husband had been with other women. I was raised the
traditional Mexican way. I was a virgin till the day I
got married. I didn't like the thought of girls that live
here in town, when they see him and if they dated him.
It bothered me that they knew him intimately. You
know, that's the way I was raised. I wanted him all to
myself, you know? He's my husband now.*

One of Tony's very first thoughts was, "Oh, my God, I'm going to die, and people are going to think I'm gay." And I reacted to that, I was very hurt, you know? I looked at him, and I said, "Why would people think you're gay?"

And he said, "Well, you know, doesn't this just happen to gay people?"

And I said, "Obviously not." You know it hit me right away that it wasn't just a gay disease, a homosexual disease. His way of thinking was, "Well, gay people deserve it. They know what they're getting themselves into." It has changed a lot the way he used to think, and he's learned a lot. I—well I should say, we both have learned a lot.

Then we had to go through the worst horror. Johnny was also HIV positive. When I had my test done, they said they were going to have to test him. I didn't care about me being positive, but I did care about the baby being positive.

Meria told me that they had just had their second baby three months before Tony tested positive for HIV. Then she said, "*We already lost a baby.*"

Two years after their marriage, Tony and Maria had their firstborn, a baby boy. They named him Tony, after his father. He lived only four months. The obituary reported that graveside services were held, but no cause of death was reported.

Meria continued the story about baby Tony.

I had to tell the doctor, "Okay, take my baby off the life support." The doctors told me, "He's just not going to make it. You're just prolonging it with the machine." So that was a very difficult decision to make.

*I had already lost a child, and it's never ever easy to
lose a child, and then I had a new baby.*

During the interview, the new baby, now twenty months old,
came toddling into the room ahead of his aunt, Meria's younger
sister. They stayed only a short time, as she stood outside the
room and then left to go in the living room with Tony. The baby
climbed onto the bed with some help. Meria and he were gleefully
jabbering away. It was touching to see him hug his mama. He
pointed to her catheter and touched it. He lost interest quickly
and went to be with his aunt and father. Meria explained:

*I've always allowed him to see my catheter. You
know, he was very curious. He's never pulled it. He
grabbed it, he looked, and you know, he said, "That
mama's owie. And I said, well, it's not an owie. He
calls an owie either a scratch or a cut or when he hurts
himself, whatever. I say, "It's not really an owie. I go,
"It's for mama's medicine, which are vitamins. But he
can't say vitamina, so he says memina. So, I say, "This
is for mommy's meminas."*

When I asked Meria, she told me the baby now lives with
his grandparents and calls his nineteen-year-old aunt, who lives
with their parents, "Mama." She said, "Tony and I visit him
four to five times a week."

Then getting back to her story about learning of Tony's
positive HIV status, she said:

*I knew I had to have AIDS. I just didn't want to
deal with it. There was a lot I felt—there was a lot that
had gone on in my life. I thought, my God, what else,
you know?*

The "what else?" is not completely knowable. Two years after the interview, I began working on the manuscript of Meria's story at Hedgebrook, a community of women writers on Whidbey Island in Langley, Washington. When I received my letter of acceptance for my residency on May 2, 1995, one of my early phone calls was to Meria. I anticipated interviewing her again, perhaps meeting her mother, and possibly seeing Johnny again. Her phone had been disconnected. I immediately phoned Judy, a social worker and my original recruiter.

Meria had died at age twenty-five on February 13, 1995. Tony had died at age twenty-eight on August 31, 1993, less than one month after our interview. I was told by Silvia, her attending nurse, that Meria had suffered a long and miserable death, filled with guilt, until a miracle, a healing of the soul, occurred in the hospital between Meria and a priest. I never learned what that was about. But it seemed that, by some miracle, according to the hospital nursing staff, Meria woke up the next morning and said, "I want to home. I am going home."

Before Tony passed away, they had a recommitment service and celebration of their marriage. Tony was not well, but was there in a white tuxedo, sat in a chair, too weak to participate. Meria wore her white wedding dress. The lace had been redesigned to cover her catheter tube. There was a ceremony, officiated by a deacon as well as the wife of the priest of the local Episcopal church. Photographs were taken, and there was a dinner and dancing at the local lodge hall. According to Silvia, the ceremony was like a first wedding. She told me, "I will always remember Meria as a bride. Even though Tony was too weak to dance, Meria was lively, and had everyone dancing to the music. The most touching event in this tremendously emotional day, was Meria dancing with Johnny, then four years old, dressed in a white tuxedo. Everyone watched as they danced together, and there was not a dry eye in the house."

Meria moved in with her mother and stepfather after that. She endured terrible pain, and her whole life was centered on looking forward to Johnny coming home from Head Start and sharing his school life and whatever pictures he had made. She lived for Johnny. According to Silvia, Meria should have let go and died, but she didn't. She hung on, through the pain, to experience another day with Johnny. She also hung on to help her family get a new house. As long as she lived with her family, there were disability benefit checks and her disability status that helped her family qualify for subsidized housing. She died shortly after the family moved into the new house.

She wanted to die at home. Her mother had doubts that she could handle her daughter's death at home, but she honored Meria's wishes. Though she had been in and out of the hospital, on her final day Meria collapsed at home. Her mother, who was described as a small, short woman, somehow picked Meria up, put her in the car, and drove to the hospital. This was a difficult task since Meria had several open sores on her back. A Franciscan friar had been called to visit another patient, but when Meria arrived, he was diverted by the staff to attend to her. The friar spoke Spanish and told the family to say their good-byes and make their peace. Marie's mother called her husband and daughters and told them to come, but to leave Johnny at home with his uncle.

Meria and her younger sister had had a falling out, about what I don't know. They had to clear it up. According to Silvia, Meria was able to say what she needed to her. And whatever the difficulty, Meria had decided that her mother and stepfather would have custody of Johnny, and not her sister.

What started out for Meria as a high school romance with Tony ended in a tragedy. A young girl marries her high school sweetheart, and they are supposed to live happily ever after, or at least have some fun trying. And in the end, a disease assumed to be far from their intended script killed Meria and Tony and the family they had created. Their son alone survived. An unintentional menacing series of events, at a time when the medical experts did not yet realize that HIV could be transmitted between monogamous heterosexual couples, led to the end of their family

Tony never intended to destroy himself, his wife, and his firstborn son. It is not as if he set out to eliminate himself and his family. But while the experts were dazed, overwhelmed, and confused by the new disease, and focused on certain risky behaviors attributed to gay men alone, Tony slipped by without recognition. Would this tragedy have been averted or altered had he been diagnosed earlier?

All Tony's sorrow, along with Meria's forgiveness, could not eliminate his guilt. There was no penance great enough, long enough, difficult enough, frightening enough to take away the guilt and erase the truth. Meria was forgiving, and at the same time took on all the responsibilities of childcare, husband care, health care, guardianship care, financial care, and death care.

What went wrong? Not only did Meria exemplify the good-girl script by saving herself for marriage, she also blamed herself while burying her firstborn son and feared her husband would leave her. She thought she had taken their baby out too soon, or perhaps his hair was wet. Then her husband was diagnosed with AIDS, and she knew that meant she had it. Only then did they realize that the first child's pneumonia was most probably due to AIDS, eventually confirmed by their physician. But Meria feared that her second son had it, too, and it turns out he did initially. However, by age two, Johnny's HIV status had reverted to negative. Meria buried her husband. And then she died an exceptionally cruel death. Yes, it's a tragedy, but her son Johnny lives.

Meria, may you rest in peace. Your mother and family care for your son. Your story is told.

Kiss from God

I was told her mark was a "kiss from God."

The small spider-like dark pattern, about the size of the head of a pen, on my daughter's right shoulder had not been there at her birth. In fact, I felt I was to blame. Perhaps it was from the time I had let her stay out in the sun too long when she was a year and a half. It was after that hot summer at the lake house when the mark appeared. It would gradually fade and disappear but then reappear when her skin was exposed to the sun.

She never talked about her mark, and I never asked her how she felt about it. I assumed she was either satisfied with the explanation that it was a "kiss from God," or she didn't think about it that much. Hopefully she didn't feel overly self-conscious about it. She was tainted with an imperfection. Or perhaps since it was not talked about, it had no prominence in her life. For whatever reasons, there was silence around the mark.

Time passed, and it was her senior prom. We shopped at Britex Fabric Store on Post Street in San Francisco for teal-blue silk for the dress she had designed. It was to have tiny spaghetti straps with a sweetheart neckline; it would be fitted carefully to her young, slim body, with the hem longer in the back, allowing the silk to both cling and flow. It would be finished with a lining of the same smooth silk, cream colored, to give shape and a soft feeling next to her skin, fashioned like the most expensive of gowns.

Though I was an experienced seamstress, the weight of the occasion for my daughter and her sweet boyfriend prompted me to suggest a professional. We chose one who'd done fine work on a black flowing dress my daughter had worn for the high school Dance Department's spring recital. She choreographed and performed her solo to a recording of Michael Bolen singing "Georgia," accompanied by piano and snare drums. Both the seamstress and my daughter earned praise for their creations.

There was joy and satisfaction going together for the fittings and then shopping for satin pumps at Nordstrom's, and rhinestone earrings, glistening but not gaudy. They were small, a diamond cut, and a perfect size for my daughter's petite face. For her lipstick and the delicate handkerchief embroidered with her grandmother's initial, she borrowed my needlepoint opera purse with various shades of pink roses and a finely textured chain. I did sew a velvet bolero jacket with three-quarter-length sleeves, to keep her bare shoulders warm in the usual foggy June nights.

This would have been the time, a young girl's senior prom, when I thought she might mention her mark. I wondered if she'd ever tried to wash it away. Why was it difficult for me to ask her about it? As close as we were, I knew that, like every young girl entering womanhood about to leave for college, there were subjects that were understood to be outside our relationship. Was this one of those subjects?

Why was I hesitant to broach the topic? I guess there were many other more practical things for us to talk about, like managing her money, washing her own clothes, and picking up her side of the dormitory room she would be sharing.

Why hadn't I asked her how she felt about the mark? Was it my guilt feelings that perhaps the mark was my fault? Was I afraid she would blame me, and that would somehow change our relationship? I doubted that. Or was it something else? Now I wonder, *Was there some wisdom in the "kiss from God"?* Who originally said this? Was it our daughter's pediatrician, Dr. Ezekiel, or her dad, a minister? Was it to alleviate any stigma or suggestion of being less than perfect? What is it about the admiration of beauty that creates for most women a sense of not being pretty enough?

Now, twenty-five years later, my daughter is a New York-based choreographer with her own dance company and married to an actor. I realize that the only contribution I made to her high school senior prom was the jacket that covered the mark.

Lift-Off

The same month I graduated with my PhD from UC San Francisco in 1992, the Columbia space shuttle was launched. But unlike that lift-off, I was still on the ground and attempting to set in motion a new career. The joy I felt in fulfilling my dream of becoming a sociologist was overshadowed by the fact that I was entering my twenty-third tenured year of teaching dental hygiene at Chabot Community College.

How could I possibly propel myself into a new career while still hanging onto the familiar but unfulfilling one? I was fifty-two. And I was beginning to dislike the part of myself that had judged other Chabot tenured faculty, like me, for staying at a job too long in various departments on campus.

I lacked confidence that I could earn money as a sociologist. However, I believed with a passion that my research on women's experience of the AIDS epidemic was an important story to be investigated and told. I was unsure that I could compete for teaching jobs in the Bay Area because of my age. I knew age discrimination was illegal, but I was realistic that I would probably not be hired at age fifty-two for a tenured position unless I was willing to relocate. Two women sociologists, a year ahead of me at UCSF and about my age, but single, had left the Bay Area for tenure track positions, one in South Dakota and the other in Detroit. That was not an option I wanted to pursue.

The UCSF faculty had painted a dismal job-search picture, telling us current graduates that 1992 was one of the worst years to get a job, and that the market was flooded with sociologists looking for work. In addition, the San Francisco Bay Area was a prime place to work and live, which made it even more competitive. I was "geographically bound" being married and living in the parsonage that was part of my minister husband's financial contract with the church he served. We had lived in our home in the Berkeley Hills since 1980 with our extended families close by. I was not prepared to change this situation, as it would leave my husband and me looking for jobs and housing when our daughter was in her first year of college in San Diego. Keeping the dental hygiene teaching position was financial security while I embarked on a new career.

I knew I was at a distinct disadvantage in the job market. I accepted this as a challenge, and I presumed my prospective employers knew that they had the advantage. But with the help of two fellow alumni from UCSF, Mary and Diane, I eventually secured some part-time teaching jobs. My hope was that getting my foot in the door would help open up further possibilities.

Mary had graduated a year before me and was continuing at her longtime teaching position in the Bay Area at St. Mary's College in Moraga, about twenty-five miles from her home in Emeryville. She was the oldest graduate student in the department. In her jovial and good-natured manner, she had shared, "I have to hurry up and graduate before I start collecting Medicare." She was generous of spirit, funny, nonjudgmental, and had a great collection of stories as an only child growing up in New York City. All through our four years together at UCSF, we met regularly for drinks at Trader Vic's, a Polynesian-style restaurant overlooking San Francisco Bay, and we talked on the phone anytime one of us needed support. We usually talked about our developing theories and ideas concerning our research, and how to maneuver the maze of grad school. Mary knew I swam regularly, so she arranged for me to use the outdoor pool at her housing complex. Even after we graduated, our friendship continued with laughter, drinks, and phone conversations, the latter focused mostly on publishing our dissertation findings, the joys and frustrations of teaching, and, in my case, looking to develop a new career. With Mary's help, I was hired to teach a research methods course at St. Mary's College, the private liberal arts school where she taught, based on her recommendation and my qualifications.

Left to my own devices, I pumped up my courage, if not my confidence, and like a salesperson, made cold calls to develop a career in my new field. I knew I did not want a tenured teaching position. In my twenty-two years' experience of teaching dental hygiene at Chabot College, tenure looked like being strapped into meetings, committee work, and revising policies that were sometimes petty. It had little to do with imparting knowledge and mentoring students, which was what I loved about teaching.

I knew more about what I *didn't* want in my new career than what I did. I was exploring new territory. Traditionally, a recent PhD went into academia on a tenure track position. So it wasn't always clear to me how to proceed on my unorthodox path. However, what I did know was that I wanted to be affiliated with a university, not a community college, teaching less than full-time, and with a large component of my contract devoted to research. I wanted to be independent with opportunities to apply for funding for my own proposals. That was what I had done for my dissertation, and I'd liked being my own boss. Dr. Barbara Gerbert at UCSF was a model for me. She taught some lectures, but primarily I knew her as the principal investigator on her funded research. This enabled her to develop a team that supported her work, and I was one of her research associates for over a year prior to beginning my doctoral training. I learned that I loved every aspect of research and interacting with the two other team members. It was rigorous, intellectually stimulating, and fun because Barbara made it that way.

However, I also knew from my experience that I did not want to be teaching and doing research at the UCSF level because of its extremely competitive nature. I had been competitive in that environment for six years, as a research associate and as a doctoral student.

Starting over at fifty-two, with the potential of fifteen or so years of working life left, I felt I had ideas I wanted to develop and get funded for new research. I wanted to continue, as I had as a graduate student, to present my work nationally, and potentially internationally, and to publish my findings. But I did not want the burden of having to "publish or perish" on the specific timetable of a tenured position, while being distracted by the university's demands that tenure required. I preferred to be an independent scholar, and to be more of a big fish in a little pond than a small fish in a big pond. So that narrowed the field of opportunities to the state universities. But clearly, I was figuring this out as I went along. I had a vision, but there were no guidelines, and I wasn't sure anyone would be willing to hire me. I didn't know how I was going to develop this career, or even if it were possible.

Without rose-colored glasses, I began my search by identifying UCSF sociology alumni in the area and where they taught. Diane was the second person, after Mary, whom I contacted. Though I had never met Diane, she agreed to meet with me in her office at California State University, Hayward, on the fourth floor of Meiklejohn Hall. Slim, attractive, and articulate, Diane was very generous with her time and advice. Like me, she had gone back for her doctorate in midlife. She shared that she had started teaching at CSUH as a lecturer and was now on the tenure track in the Sociology Department. We talked about our mutual experiences of starting a new career and research projects. Her sharing helped ease my anxiety as I was inexperienced in this "hat in hand" approach to inquiring of possible teaching opportunities.

"We don't have any openings at this time," she said. "However, with your educational background in women's issues and your research, I think you would be well suited to teach in the Women's Studies Program."

This was a novel idea and very appealing to me. I felt encouraged by her support.

She said, "Let me call Pat, the chair of the program."

Facing Diane, I sat there thinking, *What unbelievable beginner's luck.* Here she was telling Pat about my extensive qualifications with impressive teaching experience, and that I was personable and mature. I was surprised and pleased when she suggested I walk down the hall to meet Pat right away. Was that because I was coming into who I wanted to be? Was I showing up as the professional PhD graduate I was, shedding my dental hygiene teacher persona? I was pleased with the meeting, as this was my first attempt to present myself and what I had to offer to a stranger for a job.

I walked down one floor to meet Pat in her office. This tall, stunningly beautiful, African American woman with a voice that carried down the long hall and back impressed me. She intimidated me too, but I kept up my confidence by running a tape in my head: *Remember, you are Dr. Barnes*, a status that I had acquired only weeks before. Nevertheless, it helped give me self-assurance.

"We are a program and not a department," Pat said. "There are no tenured positions and probably never will be. The program is housed in the Ethnic Studies Department where the tenured faculty teaches most of the courses. But occasionally we need lecturers to fill in. Would you be interested it that?" Her voice ended on a high pitch.

Her bright eyes, her double-pierced ears with matched sets of earrings, one of gold and the other diamonds, and her purple sweater that looked hand knit, and her necklace of multiple strands of black-and-white beads all made for an impressive style. But it was her forthright approach that compelled me to want to teach in and be part of this program. She had been hired just the year before, was enthusiastic and perhaps five or six years younger than I. I liked her right away. "Yes, I'm very interested," I said. "And thank you for the opportunity to meet you."

"Well, don't thank me. Just fill out the application and return it to me as soon as possible. Then we'll see what happens."

I left feeling hopeful. Here were two dynamic women engaged in what I sensed was an intellectually electrifying environment that I longed to have in my new career. I was closer to envisioning a career as a sociologist, but the prospect of being stuck at the community college teaching dental hygiene was an ongoing worry.

As the summer's cool, foggy weather faded into our a warm September, I was preparing new course syllabi and lectures in sociology at Chabot College and research methods at St. Mary's to begin teaching in a few weeks, in addition to teaching three-quarter time in dental hygiene. I had secured one course at Chabot entitled "Introduction to Sociology." Having one foot in two different departments at Chabot, one in social science and the other in health science, was unusual. I thought it wise to keep the sociology teaching, as well as the St. Mary's teaching, in the background, especially in the Health Science Department that housed the dental hygiene program. I didn't want to appear any more unusual than I already felt. I sensed that I was looked upon as someone attempting to change my professional life, and for some colleagues that might be interpreted as being too big for my britches and too high and mighty to teach dental hygiene. There were innuendos that I would not continue to teach dental hygiene, but in reality, I barely had the potential of a sociology career. So leaving a tenured position to teach a course here and there was neither a secure move nor a wise financial choice. In my mind I was teaching sociology and research methods as a way to gain experience doing what I wanted to do, which was to teach sociology full time.

Just as I was leaving the house for a break from teaching preparations to go for a swim at Mary's outdoor pool, the phone rang. I debated letting the answering machine pick up but changed my mind.

It was Pat who, in her thunderous voice, said, "Donna, the hiring committee has reviewed your application and we would like to offer you a course in women's studies starting next Tuesday and Thursday from eight till ten forty."

I was thrilled that I was getting an offer. Then my heart sank like an aborted space shuttle launch as I realized that on those same days, at Chabot College, I had a mandatory office hour at eleven o'clock. Mandatory meant the whole college reserved this hour for meetings. There were no exceptions. With deep regret, I thanked her, explaining that the schedule would not work with my other teaching commitments.

Feeling downhearted, I drove to the outdoor pool in Emeryville, about fifteen minutes away. I let myself sink to the bottom of the Olympic size pool, immersed in the coolness. I had the whole pool to myself as I kicked off the side and began aggressive breaststrokes, moving up and down the lane in furious motion. Thinking only of the missed opportunity, I went over in my mind how I could possibly manage to teach from 8:00 to 10:40 at CSUH and within fifteen or twenty minutes get to Chabot College. It was less than four miles, but I also needed to consider the walk to and from my car at both colleges, as well as traffic and parking. Initially, I thought it too risky to try to do both, but the harder I swam, the more determined I was to try. At about the seventh lap, I swam to the side and lifted myself onto the edge of the pool. I grabbed my backpack and walked over to the pay phone on the wall of the restroom. I dug out a quarter from my wallet and from my Palm Pilot located and dialed Pat's phone number. No more than forty-five minutes had passed since I'd talked with her.

"Hello, Dr. G., this is Donna Barnes," I said. "If the offer is still open, I would very much like to teach the course."

"Well, I'm glad. Stop by the Ethnic Studies office tomorrow and see Leila, the department secretary. She'll have your paperwork ready in the afternoon for your signature. She will help you with your textbook order and a sample syllabus to assist you in compiling your own. Also, be sure to get a request for your office key. We're short on office space, so you'll be sharing an office with me. Leila will also direct you to the Human Resources Department in the Administration Building for further paperwork. You can also purchase a faculty parking permit, which is essential as parking is limited. I look forward to seeing you next week at the start of the quarter."

Thus, in less than a week, I was to begin my new career. I was ready for the challenge, like an astronaut in the Columbia space shuttle, beginning the countdown and hopeful for lift-off.

I suddenly found myself teaching three courses at three colleges within a thirty-mile radius of my home. Two days a week at six thirty in the morning I drove to CSU Hayward. After teaching there, I traveled across town for the mandatory office hour, followed by four hours of teaching clinical dental hygiene at Chabot. Leaving Chabot sometime after four, I drove thirty-two miles in traffic to St. Mary's College to teach a course at six. My friend Pat put a positive spin on my schedule by calling me a "Roads Scholar."

The two other days I drove to Chabot to teach sociology, dental hygiene, and clinic. Teaching at three colleges with three new courses—Sociology, Methods of Research, and women's studies—kept me busy. With my new career came lecture and examination preparations, grading papers, and meeting with students during office hours. In addition, it was important to me to become part of the women's studies program, beyond teaching. I also wanted to be fully prepared and present as I gave dental hygiene lectures, supervised clinic, and participated in staff and division meetings. At night I was completing a manuscript based on my dissertation for publication and applying for grants to continue my research in HIV/AIDS. My workday usually ended between two and three in the morning. This was similar to what I had been doing as a grad student. I recall one of my dissertation committee members saying, "If you think graduate school is hard, wait until you're employed."

After a year as a "Roads Scholar," I dropped the sociology course at Chabot and the research course at St. Mary's. With Pat's guidance and support, I expanded my women's studies teaching. Within two years, in the fall of 1995, I had a 60 percent contract as lecturer with benefits at CSU Hayward, teaching two courses for three quarters, with the option to teach summer school.

My women's studies teaching experience suited me, and I was happy. The students were a mixture of first generation, first time, and returning students. I could identify with them on all accounts. In a class size of fifty students, there were mostly women with perhaps a half-dozen men. The students represented a racial and ethnic diversity that was a comfortable change for me. They were motivated and generally engaged in the issues of gender, race/ethnicity, and such practical matters as discrimination in various social institutions, including employment and health care settings, because they had experienced it. The pay gap, for example, was always an eye-opener for them, an issue they found hard to reconcile.

Wanting to be prepared for students' concerns, I began investigating resources for student counseling, medical and health issues, tutoring, and individuals with disabilities. I was eventually asked to become a member of the Committee for the Student Health Center, which I gladly accepted, along with campus opportunities to give talks on HIV/AIDS prevention. At Pat's invitation, I became a member of the Women's Studies Counsel, a group of women faculty members dedicated to promoting and improving the program. The group offered support to one another, usually meeting in members' homes. I attended activities my students were involved in like theatre and dance productions, and the occasional baseball game.

It was unorthodox for a person with my credentials to not seek a tenure-track position, but not unusual as the market was flooded with job-seekers. Lecturers were considered to be less prestigious, and we were paid less than the faculty because our responsibilities were limited to teaching without requirements to do academic counseling, attend faculty or department meetings, be on curriculum development committees, be members of the governing body known as the faculty senate, or engage in research. That was more than satisfactory for me, as it allowed me to be more independent and freer to participate in ways that optimized my skills. I intended to do research, even though it was not part of my job. I had a passion to contribute to the body of knowledge about women living with HIV/AIDS. And as a sociologist interested in social institutions, I was determined to redefine and bring more respect to lectureship because it was my choice, and not a Plan B strategy for failure to get a tenured position.

At this point I was closer to my ideal job of being able to teach ideas and critical thinking, as opposed to techniques, and to be independent and not bound by required committee work, though I could volunteer selectively. What was missing was funding to develop my ideas for research to investigate social issues for women living with HIV/AIDS, specifically their access to health care, reproductive decision-making, and motherhood experiences. In order to do research, I needed grant funding. As soon as I settled into my teaching responsibilities, I got myself to the Office of Research and Faculty Development to inquire about funding.

I met Vicky, the assistant director, to inquire about research support for lecturers. Vicky was the most welcoming staff person I had yet to meet in the administration building. She wore a smile from here to Kansas and responded to my request for research funding opportunities with such enthusiasm that I felt as if I were the only person who'd ever asked about this. After a discussion about my research interests, she promised to have a list of potential grant sources emailed to me.

It was my commitment to interview women with HIV/AIDS, still a marginalized group within the AIDS epidemic. Even though this was not a requirement for lecturers, I could not conceive of turning my back on what I felt was an important social issue to bring to light. So I applied for funding and received a fellowship from the National Endowment for the Humanities to study at Boston University for the summer of 1994. I was one of eleven fellows studying "Morality and Society." Though this fellowship paid my salary and housing, it did not supply me with funds to interview women, something I felt zealous about. I insisted on being able to offer women I interviewed an honorarium, as they were experts in their experience of living with HIV/AIDS. What this fellowship did provide, however, was the opportunity to read philosophy and to further extend my dissertation research on disclosure under the leadership of Dr. Alan Wolfe and the other fellows. Dr. Wolfe asked me to lead a discussion in how private disclosure decisions of potentially stigmatizing information such as HIV status are a public health issue. I was in my element receiving Dr. Wolfe's support. This experience helped sharpen my skills as a scholar.

Doors were opening but also colliding. Returning from Boston to CSU Hayward in the fall of 1995, I began teaching on my renewable contract with benefits. With this potential financial security, I resigned from teaching dental hygiene at Chabot Community College effective December 31, 1995. Then the collision happened. I received a letter from the University of Illinois at Chicago stating that I had been awarded a six-month paid post-doctorate residency with health benefits that would begin in January 1996 in Chicago. The John D. and Catherine T. MacArthur Foundation would fund my proposed research on the experience of women with HIV/AIDS deciding on their reproductive decisions, and who if anyone they talked to about it. This was my second application for this residency; my first had been denied, but with an invitation to apply again. I felt elated, but in a dilemma. How could I do the residency without losing my new, coveted CSU Hayward contract?

Pat was immediately enthused. She congratulated me and offered an instant solution. Her advice was to start my teaching contract in the fall and later tell the dean, who would recognize the residency as a prestigious award for both me and CSU Hayward. On Pat's advice, I could request a leave of absence without pay, and accept the pay and health benefits attached to the UIC offer. I took her advice and when I returned from Chicago, my contract was still in place.

Pat was a terrific boss and became a longtime friend. She was supportive of my research activities, encouraged me to develop a new course, and bolstered my teaching position within the faculty by inviting me to meetings and social functions for the program. Her spirit of generosity made it possible for me to blossom in the position, though at one point in our sixteen-year association, she told me she never thought her legacy would be to support a white woman. I liked her forthright and honest approach.

I was not always smoothly circling the universe in my space shuttle. In my second year of teaching women's studies, I had an experience that set me back. I had been invited by the president of CSU Hayward to attend a meeting with select women faculty and other community women of influence to discuss female faculty's needs. The invitation was unusual, as I suspected that I was the only lecturer in the room. I was honored and felt like I was finally launched as a sociologist and had buried my past. For sure, I was intimidated as I entered the president's spacious, top floor office in the tallest building on campus, with carpeted floors and a wall of windows overlooking the bay. I recognized only a few women, Pat being one of them. As I moved into the gathering, I was stunned to hear a woman in a loud high-pitched voice coming from the crowd say, "Donna, my dental hygienist. What are you doing here?" She was laughing as she walked toward me. It was as if a military tank had come across the room to flatten me.

As hard as I had worked to achieve my new status as Dr. Barnes, I was humiliated as I looked around the room of faces staring at me as if I had a scarlet letter on my breast. I wanted to say to this former patient, "I am not your or anyone's dental hygienist." But that would have made me look and feel even smaller. I don't recall much of the meeting feeling I was not worthy to be there. Whether the group continued to meet, I don't know. I do know that I didn't receive another invitation. Pat and I never talked about it because I felt too awkward and embarrassed to bring it up. I learned from this episode that you may bury the past, but it can be hard to keep it buried.

However, after I returned from the University of Illinois at Chicago in the summer of 1997, major launching happened. With my contract affiliation with CSU Hayward, and based on my research findings at UIC, I applied for federal grant money from the National Institutes of Health (NIH). I proposed to build on my investigation of women with HIV/AIDS's reproductive decision experiences by adding two more sample sites. Besides Chicago, I proposed to include Rochester, New York, and Oakland, California. It took me two rounds of submission of my proposed research before I received the first of twelve years of continuous NIH funding in the fall of 1997.

I had job security now at CSU Hayward in the form of a three-year renewable contract with benefits, and research funding on a four-year renewable application cycle. With this support I became the principal investigator on projects I proposed that paid my salary, bringing my income to full-time. The NIH funding included a budget that paid my interviewees and my travel expenses to my two sample sites. I established a bicoastal paid research team consisting of a research associate housed in my now private office at CSUH, multiple recruiters, and four consultants, two at each site. Over the twelve years, I had three projects studying social issues for women with HIV/AIDS and the providers who cared for them.

What was especially wonderful, and part of the mandate of these grants, was that I mentored underrepresented students into doctoral programs. I hired CSUH master's degree graduate students as my research associates. After they left to begin their PhD programs, we continued our friendships. I helped mentor some of them into the job market and four of them were coauthors for academic publications based on our research. This felt particularly satisfying as a way to pay back those who had assisted me in my journey.

In 2009, I retired from CSU Hayward. I write full-time in my home study, both academic and creative writing on my own schedule. Particularly relevant, I put my needs first, or at minimum, on a par with my husband and family's needs. In truth, I did not have the necessary educational skills and emotional support I thought I needed for creating a new career as a sociologist in midlife. Nor did I have the training to embark on the path to become a writer/artist. Interestingly, both jobs were suggested as most suitable to me from career counseling I had in 1987 based on multiple personality tests. Ultimately, I found support in my family; first and foremost from my daughter and my sister, as well as three longtime female friends, alumnae from my creative writers' residencies, and select UCSF faculty and alumni.

What I have learned is to listen and pay close attention to my instincts and attempt to silence my inner critic. It is important, I have found, to protect myself from negative people, all the while attempting to be kind to everyone. Many wise women have been my guides and supports. Some have been major, like my daughter, Diane, Mary, and Pat, and others have taken the time to offer a sentence or two in relatively minor interactions with major results. I am thinking of the woman employee at CSU Hayward Foundation where I took one of my grant proposals for a signature. She looked at the title, asked me a few questions and said, "You need to meet Dr. Maria Nieto. Let me call her, and you take this over to her and find out how to apply for the NIH funding." That led me on a fruitful path.

Looking back I know that I risked job and financial security for an unknown career as a sociologist. I've experienced some bumps along the way, but perseverance gave rise to creativity and joy. After shedding my cocoon of security, I learned that by letting go of my fear of what I might lose, I opened myself up to far-reaching opportunities and challenges I had never considered, even in my most cockeyed dreams.

Hedgebrook

I applied to Hedgebrook, a community of women writers on Whidbey Island, Washington. The residency included a cottage of one's own, all meals provided, walks in the woods, and bicycles. The day I received my acceptance, I cried.

What inspired me most at Hedgebrook was that I was honored as a writer. More important than what I produced was finding my rhythm that developed into my writing practice. That was the most valuable thing I took home. I learned that as a writer, I needed uninterrupted time and a room of my own to write my insights, my story. In my cottage with the door closed, I was challenged without responsibilities. I learned to honor my writing practice and discovered it needed to be supported by good food, the generosity of a reciprocal relationship of writers, and my families and friends. Nancy Nordhoff taught me, by her example, to honor nature and the necessity of spending time in the outdoors, to breathe the air, relax the body, and refresh the spirit.

Occasionally Victoria and I went swimming in Gross Lake, which felt rejuvenating. One of the writers had her family visit for the day. On the sparse beach, her son said, loud enough that I could hear, "That writer sure is a strong swimmer." I was more flattered that he called me a writer than by being admired for my swimming.

When I felt stuck in my writing or needed in an idea, I rode the #4 blue bicycle past the farmhouses to the beach. At times I woke before dawn and biked, turning left up the hill into the sunrise. What a way to greet the day with renewed challenges and possibilities for my writing and myself. Every day I would walk in the woods or go to the beach to refresh my mind and body. The library in Freeland was also a bike ride away. There, as a Hedgebrook resident, I could check out books and music cassettes.

One night I was listening to Ella Fitzgerald while I painted. Another evening I listened in the bathtub to Maya Angelou reading *I Know Why the Caged Bird Sings*, and later sat on the window seat to look at the stars.

One July full moon, apparently the largest of the year, Theresa, Victoria, and I traveled about forty minutes to Ehy's Landing to get the best view to watch the sunset and the moonrise. Theresa said it was a special event, and that we should make a wish on this exceptional night.

We didn't speak but just walked on the beach. I made a wish that my inner wisdom would be aligned with my outer actions. No more saying and doing what others expected of me. I wanted integrity for myself. We drove home mostly in silence, keeping our wishes to ourselves.

Most nights the writers gathered in the library. Usually two people read their work in progress, and others listened and

gave feedback in a supportive and honest way. The feedback
I received that was most helpful was that one character in the
story was naked and exposed, the woman in the white Volvo.
I wanted to know more about her. It was not easy to expose
myself, but each reading and feedback session was like a course
in creative writing. With my Hedgebrook sisters' help, I shed
the objective sociologist's gaze and looked at the world as a
vulnerable person with feelings, hopes, and fears. I was like a
sinner who had been reborn a novice creative writer. I had a
long way to go, but I was on the path of salvation. Praise the
Lord or Goddess. Hell, why not praise both?

As the days passed, I quickly realized that there was an unspo-
ken respect for who I was in this place from Hedgebrook founder
Nancy Nordhoff, to Denise the cook, the staff, and the gardener.
I felt admiration and warmth from the other writers, especially
Theresa and Victoria. I was embracing myself as the writer.

Toward the end of my three weeks, Theresa offered
to do a tarot card reading. My only former experience with the
psychic world had been in London at the College of Psychic
Studies where I'd had a reading. I was on sabbatical and studying the health care delivery system. In Great Britain I found that
the spiritual world was not as separate from the medical world
as it was in the US at that time.

Theresa interpreted my life pattern as laid out in the cards.
The next morning, as I listened and transcribed the reading,
the tarot cards showed, according to Teresa, that I was in an
unorthodox period.

She told me, "It is a time for yourself where no one is going
to distract you."

People can take it or leave it. You have no choice.

Teresa interpreted that the reason for my eagerness to focus
on myself was that if I don't, I will feel like my father who did

the noble thing of working at a job that provided economic stability but that was below his intellectual potential. I had never heard Dad complain about his job; on the contrary, he was proud, as I was of him, for studying for tests that improved his work prospects and therefore his income over the years.

However, Theresa's interpretation for me was frighteningly true. I was working at a job that I had known for several years was no longer intellectually satisfying.

But I stayed for economic reasons that included our family's medical and dental insurance. I especially did not want my reduced income to affect our daughter's choice of college. We agreed that she should not be burdened by financial responsibility as an undergraduate. We wanted her to be able to choose freely without finances being the primary consideration.

Another of Teresa's bull's eyes was when she said, "The feeling you have to prove your intellect comes from your sense of having to fake it. You thought the only way to get anything was to sneak around."

That made so much sense. I was aware that I was frequently making it up as I went along.

She said, "This came from not having the necessary skills. That's over." I heard this as a command, her voice loud and clear. I was ready to let go of proving myself.

Then Theresa offered counsel and advice. She cautioned, saying, "There are three things to watch for. One is to cut out all the negative and unsupportive people, the deepest of which is your own doubtful voice. When you hear, police it. It does not serve you going out in the world. It's over, played out."

Teresa was saying what I knew to be true but was unable to verbalize and act on.

"The second is that it's important that you do only what feels right. You have so much energy but be cautious and selective. Take it slow. You don't have to take any work that is not your truth. You will only sabotage yourself."

I felt her interpretation of the tarot cards was giving me permission to put myself in primary control of my work life and deal with the burden of staying at an unsatisfying job that provided health care and paid well.

Teresa continued, "The third is don't worry about the money. Don't feel pressure about it. If need be, take out a loan. Don't feel indebted. Feel good about all you have done. Practice self-compassion."

The experience of the tarot card reading was powerful, unbelievably accurate, and reassuring. It also lifted the weight about my financial responsibilities to our family, knowing there were other ways to handle our finances. She had given me the advice that my parents had not been able to do.

Within days of leaving Hedgebrook, I resigned from teaching dental hygiene, knowing I had already stayed at the job too long. Securing a contract position at California State University, Hayward, where I had a part time lectureship. I applied for federal grant money from the United States National Institute of Medical Science, and was funded for research that launched my career and secured a full-time position.

Without a doubt, I know that it was Nancy Nordhoff's support, my Hedgebrook residency, and the women who shared that experience with me that led me to change my work and my lifestyle.

Everybody Has Been
So Nice to Me

After Mom's death in 1989, Dad returned to a full life of visiting family and friends, playing golf, and maintaining our childhood home and garden. Golf was his primary challenge and joy. In 1992, he was featured in an article in the *Napa Valley Register* with the headline, "This Golfer Shoots His Age: Brazzi, 85, Loves the Challenges That the Game of Golf Presents." In the text Dad was quoted as saying, "I don't shoot my age too often." He had also shot a hole in one, about which he noted, "Everybody, regardless of who you are, is surprised to see someone get a hole in one because it is rare." I think he was being modest, as this was his fifth hole in one. Dad had earned the nickname, "Super senior golfer."

Dad played in several local golf tournaments and at times was a marshal at PGA golf tournaments held in Napa. These events ended in dinners with his friends. The local Italian Catholic Federation held dinner dances at St. John's Catholic Church that Dad attended with Mom until her death.

One day, Dad was sitting on a stool at his favorite coffee shop when Amy came in and asked, "May I sit here?" Dad recognized her as the widow of one of his best friends and golfing partners. He eventually invited Amy to dinner.

As time passed, they visited one another, had dinners together, and enjoyed drives in the Napa Valley. Dad always drove, as Amy had never learned how.

On the Friday before Thanksgiving in 1999, Dad had an episode with his driving that changed his lifestyle. He was just short of his ninety-third birthday when he became confused about finding his way home. He parked his car too far from the curb on Jefferson Street, knocked on the door of the closest house, and asked to use the phone. He called a cab to take him home.

Dad then called his younger brother, my Uncle Bill, and told him that his car was on Jefferson Street. Uncle Bill called my brother, the youngest among us at fifty-three, who drove up the next day, Saturday morning.

When he arrived, Dad was confused and upset because he couldn't remember where the car was. My brother called the police to report the car missing. The officer on the phone said, "Why do you let a ninety-two-year-old man drive?"

My brother replied, "Because the State of California renewed his license for five years when he was ninety-one."

Later that day, a friend found Dad's car by happenstance. The seats were wet as the windows had been left partially open, and it had rained.

The episode led to a gathering of the siblings that same afternoon.

On that Saturday afternoon before Thanksgiving, my brother, two older sisters, and I sat around the kitchen table with Dad in our childhood home. We were prepared to tell him it was time to give up his license and stop driving. Dad was, as always, happy to see us. He seemed to be his old self, pleasant and rational with no obvious signs of confusion. As we settled ourselves, the mood was tense, relieved somewhat by the comfort of our mugs of hot coffee and the tranquil sound of rain on the roof and the patio.

It is hard to recall how the meeting started, but certain questions were posed, and the emotions are clear in my recollection. One of my three siblings started the conversation by saying something like, "Dad, we think it's time you should stop driving."

Dad said, "I'm not sure I agree, but I'll listen to what you have to say."

The discussion went on with each of us speaking about the dangers of his driving. I pointed out, in his defense, that Dad had not had an accident or citation for many years. "Are there some restrictions to Dad's driving that would make all of us feel better about it?" I asked. I knew from experience that my oldest sister, age sixty-three, would be likely to challenge me, but she surprised me by ignoring me.

Instead, she asked Dad, "What if you were in an accident and killed someone?"

In a calm voice, Dad said, "That could happen to any of you as well."

Dad was not resisting the idea, but clearly was not yet ready to relinquish his license. At some point, my younger brother, Gary, became adamant, rising from his chair and expressing his opinion in a louder voice than necessary. I felt uncomfortable that my brother seemed to be taking some pleasure in his demand for Dad to stop driving. Maybe there was some unfinished business between the two of them.

My middle sister, only eighteen months older than I, was listening with respect. Always the peacemaker, she said, "Dad, you could take the bus or call a cab when you want to go to the Buttercream Bakery for breakfast, or to Amy's for a visit. Amy takes the bus all the time, and she can come visit you here, too. I can take you to get the bus schedule and we can take the bus together for a trial run. Wouldn't that be fun, Dad?"

I let the conversation unfold, knowing the last thing any of us wanted was a nasty argument. The situation was already delicate and difficult.

I watched as Dad gradually accepted the decision. It was his nature to avoid disagreements. After listening to each of us, he said, "I don't want to stop driving, but if you think that is the best, I will go along with it."

Dad never took the bus or a cab. Four days later, on Thanksgiving Day, he took a ride in the ambulance to the emergency room.

Again the siblings gathered to be with Dad that day. He was tested from nine in the morning until nine-thirty at night with negative results. He was sent home with instructions to see a urologist. It became clear to my siblings and me that Dad needed twenty-four-hour care. My siblings agreed that each of us would take one day a week to be with Dad. On the other three days of the week, we would hire a caretaker. When I came for my shift, Dad would say, "It makes me happy that you come to relax and visit. I know how hard you work." He seemed to think that I needed the rest, not that he needed our care. I went along with that assumption.

Most of the time, Dad was in wonderful spirits when I visited him, but his memory was failing, and he had given up golf. He said he couldn't drive the ball as well as he used to. Amy still came by bus to visit regularly. And I enjoyed driving them out to lunch or up the Napa Valley. Once we went to see an iris farm in full bloom in Napa that was only open to the public for two days. We had a picnic lunch in the sunshine.

It was a pleasure to be with Dad. Driving from my teaching job in Hayward around four in the afternoon, I'd arrive in Napa to relieve my sister, who had been with Dad since the previous day. As evening fell, I prepared dinner and set the table in the dining room with flowers from his garden: lilacs, camellias, irises, gardenias, whatever was in season. Unfailingly, he would say, "Honey, you bring a woman's touch to the home." We enjoyed our meals together. I often made beef stew with onions, carrots, and potatoes, one of his favorite meals, though he was eating less, and he gave up drinking wine with dinner as the months passed.

Whether we verbalized it or not, I felt we had been close all my life. My siblings acknowledged in our adult years that I was and had always been "Daddy's little girl." It was my joy to be his daughter. He was my model of a good person because he treated everyone with kindness and respect, and he had an easy sense of humor.

Dad was an old-world gentleman, always opening the car door, offering his arm while walking, and positioning himself on the outside for protection from traffic. In his early nineties, he still walked upright and with a purpose, not in an old person's shuffle. I never heard him swear, though I was told later by some of my cousins and uncles that it was because I had never been on a hunting or fishing trip with him.

I was proud to be with him in public as he had many friends and acquaintances who greeted us. Usually these encounters were accompanied by laughter, the kind of ribbing that comes easily with old cronies. A typical comment from Ralph, one of Dad's golfing buddies would be: "Romi, you've been retired for how many years?"

"Since 1967, that's about thirty-seven years," Dad would reply with a twinkle in his eye.

"You've been retired longer than you worked. For Christ's sake, Romi, you're the reason we have a national debt." Ralph and Dad would be slapping each other on the back and laughing.

On our weekly visits after dinner, Dad and I would sit in the living room and talk. We didn't watch television, but sometimes I played records from Mom and Dad's collection of big band sounds from the thirties and forties: Harry James, Benny Goodman, and Glenn Miller.

I loved to hear the story of Dad's voyage in 1918 from Switzerland to America to be reunited with his father, who had arrived in 1912 to earn enough money for the family's trip. Dad was eleven when he left Gudo, Switzerland, with his thirty-nine-year-old mother, his fifteen-year-old brother, Joe, his twin brother, a younger sister of nine, and a baby brother of six. They left their tiny village in the Italian part of Switzerland in the foothills of the Swiss Alps.

Imagine a mother with five children leaving behind her birth family and knowing she would never see them again. My grandmother had never heard or spoken a word of English. Giving up the security of this agricultural village, she and her children sailed across the ocean during World War I, when German submarines were a threat to civilian as well as military ships. They left the continent on November 3, 1918, and arrived at Ellis Island eight days before the fighting in World War I came to an end, following the signing of the armistice.

Dad recalled the excitement of seeing the Statue of Liberty. However, they were all quarantined in the Ellis Island hospital for several weeks because Dad's little brother had the measles or mumps. After some time, the family was released from Ellis Island and traveled west by train. Dad told me about seeing his first cowboy riding a horse as the train passed through Texas.

One Thursday, Dad talked about his admiration for his older brother, Joe. I always knew how much Dad admired his brother, who had died of tuberculosis at age thirty-two, a few days before Christmas in 1935. He had been married only a month or so. On one particular night after dinner, Dad opened his wallet to show me the photo of Uncle Joe standing next to an airplane he'd built while living with the family in Napa Junction. I didn't recall ever having seen this photo. I learned that night that Dad carried it in his wallet and had for a long time.

On yet another Thursday night, Dad told the story of when his family arrived in Napa Junction in 1918 and how they were all soon enrolled in grammar school, except for Uncle Joe, beginning in the first grade since they did not know English. When he graduated from the eighth grade, Dad was seventeen.

Upon the family's arrival, a neighbor, also an immigrant, gave Dad a baseball mitt. Of course, Dad knew nothing of the American sport, but quickly learned from the neighbors. In grammar school, Dad told me, he became the pitcher and his twin the catcher. Though their school could not afford equipment like a catcher's mask, he was proud that they beat Hunter, a more affluent school, nine to six.

Baseball soon became his favorite sport. In my growing-up years, some of my happiest memories are sitting in the grandstands behind home plate with my siblings on warm summer evenings. Shelling and eating peanuts added to the enjoyment. A favorite baseball photo dated 1929 sits on my desk. It is of the Mare Island's "Electrical Shop" fourteen-member integrated baseball team, with flannel uniforms, most matching, some not. Dad is kneeling, holding his mitt, next to the one African American player in the front row.

In my journal during our Thursdays together, I recorded that I had driven Dad through the Napa Valley on the Silverado Trail. When we stopped for lunch in Yountville, I asked Dad about his life. I was curious about what he thought of his life in America and of my grandfather's hard work to bring his family here. I wrote in my journal that night what my dad said: "I'll never be ashamed to look back. I'll never forget what my dad did for us. It makes me happy to look back. No regrets. I'd do it all over the same."

In June of 2004, after grading finals and turning in my grades, I flew to Laguna Beach, California, to be with my husband. It was the beginning of my quarter break, and I planned to stay for five days. He was employed as the interim minister at a local community church. Working in separate cities was new for us, so we tried to be together at least once a month or so.

An added bonus on this trip was to see our daughter performing a choreographed modern dance piece in San Diego. She and her husband, who flew out to join us and visit his family, lived in New York City.

On the Sunday before I left, I had visited Dad, who was in the hospital. It had been several years since that Thanksgiving ambulance trip, but recently he'd been in and out of the hospital for urinary tract infections that resisted antibiotics, and at other times for abdominal pains. On one visit to the emergency room, the attending physician determined that Dad needed exploratory surgery. This was frustrating because Dad was ninety-seven. My sisters and I felt it was too much to put him through surgery. When I tried to reason with the physician, literally following him from bed to bed in the overflow room of the emergency room, he turned to me and said, "If we don't do the surgery, your father will die." I had no response to such a threatening statement.

So when my middle sister called, I was on the alert. She said, "The doctor wants Dad to have hospice, but there is a concern that he could pass in the ambulance on the way home. So the doctor arranged for Dad to stay in the hospital."

In a moment, Dad's situation had gone from the occasional trip to the emergency room to deadly serious. Of course, I knew this was inevitable, but it still came as a surprise.

I said, "I'll book the next flight. I'll be there today. But oh, Sis, I'm not sure I'm ready for this."

"I know, but we can do this, little sister. I'll meet you at the hospital."

The second I got off the phone, my daughter said, "Mom, I'm coming with you."

Ken said that I probably shouldn't go, it was late at night, and they likely wouldn't let me go in to see him.

There was no one else I would rather have by my side at this time. But Monica had more than a full-time job as artistic director of her dance company. She and her husband were scheduled to leave the next day for New York.

"Sweetheart, are you sure you can afford the time away from your work?"

"Mom, I always knew I would be with you when Pampo was near his end. There's no doubt in my mind. Work can wait," she said.

My tears over losing Dad were mixed with tears of relief to have my daughter with me. My husband stayed in Laguna Beach, as he was an interim minister at the San Rafael Church.

Within three hours, my daughter and I were at Dad's hospital bedside, joining my two sisters, my nephew, an uncle, and a cousin. The attending nurse told us that Dad was sleeping most of the time and spoke very little. Amazingly, however, he woke up while we were all there, looked around the room, and without missing a beat, said, "Where did all these beautiful people come from?"

Laughter followed as we watched in surprise while he entertained us with comments.

"Nice haircut," he said to my nephew, who had a Michael Jackson hairdo.

"Monique, how did you get here from New York City?"

Dad liked to refer to our daughter Monica as "Monique," and he attempted a Brooklyn accent when saying New York City. It always got a laugh.

"I'm the luckiest guy in the world to have all of you here," he said.

We stayed until Dad fell asleep, maybe less than half an hour. Later we came to understand that episodes of lucidity are not unusual in the dying process.

My daughter became the caretaker for me and my siblings for the next three days. She did most of the driving to Napa. When Monica and I arrived, my sisters had come the night before. My brother and his partner arrived the next day, having driven from their home in Palm Springs.

Monica and I did the grocery shopping and fixed dinner with help from my sisters. We uncorked the wine each evening as we enjoyed being in Dad's home. Later at night, Monica drove the two of us to our home in Kensington, about an hour away, to sleep and return the next morning.

Certainly, she didn't need to be the one taking on these tasks, but it was her nature to be emotionally and physically present when our family or one of her close friends were in need. Of course, I could have driven myself back and forth to the hospital, but it was a luxury not to have to think about which turn to make on the half-hour drive, or what floor Dad was on, or what to fix for dinner. I always knew my daughter would be there for me when I needed her. "Honey," I said, "thank you for being here. You are and have always been such a support and a great caretaker for me and my siblings."

"I learned from the best, Mom."

The day after my daughter and her husband, David, returned to New York, I drove to the hospital in the late afternoon and joined my middle sister in Dad's room. We were on either side of Dad's bed as he slept, each holding one of his hands, and talking softly. The attending physician walked in as the sun was setting and darkness began closing into the room. He was kind and not in any hurry to leave, an atypical hospital experience for me. During our conversation about Dad's condition, sensing that the end was near, I said to the doctor, "I want to stay and not leave Dad's side. I know that's not practical, but it's how I feel."

He said, "This is understandable. In my experience I have seen patients hang on because they don't want to leave when a family member is present. So many deaths occur late at night or at two or three in the morning. Let me assure you that your dad will die peacefully. If one had a choice, renal failure is the best way to go. His kidneys will shut down, followed by his breathing and his heart. It is death without pain."

That gave me comfort, but I still had mixed feelings about leaving. As my sister and I said our good-byes in the hall, I decided to stay for a moment alone with Dad. I went back into his room. Though he was still asleep, I leaned down close to his ear, and said, "Dad, is there anything you want to say?"

I'm not sure what I was expecting to hear, but I wanted him to know he could die, and I wanted to offer him a chance to verbalize that he was ready. I was on a fool's errand, perhaps, but I wanted to try to ease his imminent departure.

After a few moments passed without a response, I moved my face closer to his ear. As I watched Dad with his eyes closed, and with tears rolling down his cheeks, he whispered, "Everybody has been so nice to me."

Driving home I treasured those words and renewed my vow to be more like Dad. Pulling into my garage, I wondered what it would be like to wake up some day in a world without him.

Dad died that night at 11:15 pm. He was ninety-seven years old. His last words to me, possibly to anyone, were, "Everybody has been so nice to me."

Take Action

Toward the last days of my two-week artists' residency at Ragdale in the fall of 2005, I decided to come clean to the other artists. *The New York Times* front-page news of Hurricane Katrina shook us all with the deaths and devastation of the most vulnerable neighborhoods of New Orleans. It was one of five deadliest hurricanes in the history of the United States. This tragedy made my problems seem small-minded. Yet, it had the effect on me that life was precious and short, and it demanded my honesty in this intimate setting.

Six writers, three visual artists, and one composer had gathered in the living room of the former summer home of architect Howard Van Doren Shaw. It was considered one of the finest examples of Arts and Crafts architecture in America. The large living room with wooden beam ceilings, stone fireplace, and overstuffed couches and club chairs invited relaxation after dinner. Most of the group drank wine. We saved the bourbon for later as the hardcore among us, of which I was one, stayed up talking past midnight.

In the evenings it was routine for one or two writers to read their work for critique. We did the same for the other artists, seeing or hearing their work in their studios on the property, edged by the prairie in Lake Forest, Illinois. This evening I had read from a chapter entitled, "Secrets and Integrity," part of a nonfiction book in progress. Writing about someone else's secret was easier for me than confessing my own.

At the end of the lively feedback, I said, "I have avoided disclosing two simple facts about myself. One is that I am married to a minister. The second is that I was a dental hygienist and dental hygiene instructor for thirty-three years. And I can defend why I kept this information to myself."

These were secrets I was used to keeping, having held them close many times in other contexts. It was apparent today how much I also often felt the need to defend having kept them secret. In my experience, "minister's wife" generally implied that I was an extension of my husband, and my previous work as a dental hygienist implied that I was handmaiden to a dentist, both considered subservient roles.

I was paid nothing for the first role while expected to please the congregation, or at least not to offend anyone. For some, there was an unspoken assumption that I would volunteer to serve the church. And in the second role, I was beholden to the dentist and his decisions, while doing most of the behind-the-scenes support and dirty work. In the late sixties, this was the norm for "women's work."

Frankly, the other artists were more enthusiastic about my writing than my secrets. Later, when we night owls turned to bourbon, Josie, the poet, offered to do Tarot card readings. After my reading, she asked me, "Why do you feel the need to hide your past occupation and your role as minister's wife, and to defend yourself?"

What perhaps wasn't apparent to her was that throughout my adult life, these two roles had led people to make certain assumptions about me. In reaction to that, over the years, I had built up a defense that grew larger until I did two things. First,

I began creating a new career by entering a doctoral program in sociology in 1987 at age forty-six, and second, I quit dental hygiene in 1995 at age fifty-four. Those eight years were fraught with emotional uncertainties about my success and concern about implications for our family.

What happened at Ragdale in 2005 with my public confession was supported by other writers and artists, graduate students, professors, women living with HIV/AIDS, my female friends, and most especially my daughter. At Ragdale I made a conscious decision not to live with these secrets or to play an assumed role of minister's wife.

And I claimed the quality of integrity like a soft mantle I had earned the hard way, but one that could be passed on from woman to another.

The Writer

How did he know I was a writer? He passed me in that part of New York City where the buildings are no more than four or five stories tall and in the mornings the streets are quiet. Except, that is, for the giggling young women vying to have their photograph taken on the steps of Sarah Jessica Parker's brownstone from the series, *Sex in the City*.

The man who passed me looked like he had not slept all night. He wore baggy jeans and a dark, wrinkled, hooded sweatshirt two sizes too big; he was weaving when he stepped off the curb. As he ambled past me, he said, "Write a story with me in it."

Did I look like a writer? What does a writer look like? Was the West Village so overgrown with writers that it was a safe guess? Did he use this line on every woman he passed? Was he high, drunk, perceptive, clairvoyant? It didn't matter. I felt somehow lighter, happier; his comment gave me momentary confidence.

Or maybe it was New York City. It was my dream life, walking the West Village, pretending I lived here. If I did, I would get up early every day and go to my favorite café to write for two to three hours, which is exactly what I was doing that day.

It was 2010, and I was back in New York. I had lived for a year with my husband in Hoboken, New Jersey, from 2008 to 2009. We were there because my husband had been called to be an interim minister in Montclair for eighteen months. My daughter now lived in the West Village. Hoboken was certainly not my dream residence, but I regularly took the PATH subway under the Hudson River during that year to write in the city, heading to my usual writing spot at my favorite café. At that time, it was a tiny space called MoJo Coffee on Charles Street, close to the Hudson. The tables were cut rounds of redwood trees with bark edges, secured to the floor by smaller tree stumps. They were just big enough for my laptop computer. I preferred the corner window ledge with pillows, but I was grateful for any table.

Upon my arrival, my favorite waiter, Dominick, faithfully greeted me with a lavish smile, asked about my daughter the dancer, and made me the best grilled cheese sandwich with onions and tomatoes I'd ever had. By contrast, the moody, long-haired barista could not be depended on to make me feel welcome, but he did know my drink—decaf Americano—without asking.

The close proximity of the tables made it easy to overhear conversations, many of which proved instructional. Young women spilled their guts about their previous night's adventure. Short, fat men discussed the opera, ballet, or theatre. As often as not, they were actors, directors, or producers rather than audience members. There was one older man everyone seemed to know. Was he an agent, writer, actor? I never was able to figure it out, but I enjoyed the intrigue.

I romanticize the writer's life, a routine of sitting in a favorite café where no one knows you, a place where you can be alone but part of an interesting group of anonymous people. Is it an image from Hemingway's *A Moveable Feast* that captures this idealized writer's life in Paris? This book has had an influence on me, and I desire a similar writer's life, but without the alcohol. Or is it that I crave being alone in a crowd, away from marriage and household responsibilities?

Over the years, I have been the one in our marriage who has managed our finances, home maintenance and repairs, travel, and social life. I do the cooking, and my husband does the cleanup. As the years passed, he has assumed more household chores like grocery shopping, doing his own laundry, taking out the garbage, and occasional yard work. Whenever I have asked him for help, like going to the recycling center, he does so in his pleasant and steady manner. I've not jumped over the moon in joy with this progress of sharing household responsibilities, but I have been grateful.

Many months later, I returned to New York City without my husband to complete interviews in Rochester with women with HIV/AIDS and their disclosure experiences. Several women spoke of stigmatization upon disclosing. After completing the interviews, I stayed in a small hotel in the West Village for a week to review the interviews and write up my analysis. Listening to the interviews helped me consider the themes that emerged and how to best present their stories in my writing.

I found MoJo's no longer suited me. Dominick still recognized me and asked about my daughter—and the grilled cheese was still excellent, toasted medium dark brown, fried in butter, served hot with melted cheese hanging out the sides. But the place did not charm me the way I remembered.

Without unpacking my gear, I set off to find another place to write, carrying my black bag with my laptop, a red folder with my essay of the moment; white-lined tablets; three pens, a black, extra-fine-point Sharpie, two uni-ball pens, one black and the other red; and a small pad of yellow stickies. I walked about five blocks to Café Minerva, a place discovered by my daughter. It opened at seven o'clock, allowing me to be one of the first to secure a place next to the large windows, where I was warmed by the sunshine. The tables were big enough for both my laptop and my decaf Americano, which I savored in the glow of my screen. When I got hungry, the toasted country bread from Sullivan Street Bakery, slathered with butter and honey, satisfied my taste.

For the next several days, I wrote there with a feeling of satisfaction. Seldom did I talk to anyone, except perhaps the waitperson, but then only briefly. "Good morning. Yes, please, a decaf Americano." I liked the anonymity of the big city. I was there to write, not chat.

There was one exception, however.

One Sunday morning, I had planned to get out of bed and be at Café Minerva when it opened, but I woke up at two in the morning with a sore throat. *Damn it*, I thought. I turned over and went back to sleep, rising later than planned.

I arrived at the café at close to nine and found a man in his early sixties sitting at my favorite table. With the morning sun streaming in, especially nice on this cold fall morning with the leaves flying by, I was perturbed to not have my usual spot.

The friendly waitperson, her braided hair falling to her mid-back, welcomed me.

I said, "I'm trying to decide where to sit, and my brain isn't quite functioning yet." I was thinking, *Why didn't I get up earlier?*

I settled at a table close to the man so I could easily move over when he left. Trying not to be too envious, I set up my computer and ordered my usual decaf Americano. I opened my laptop, pulled out my writing pad and pens, and got to work. Sometime later, I was caught by a sneeze as I drew a Kleenex from my vest pocket. The man turned to me and said, "Bless you."

In the conversation that followed, he introduced himself as "Michael" and asked what I was doing. When I answered, he launched into a barrage of questions: What was I writing? Was it fiction or nonfiction? What had I published? Where had I published? Where was I going to publish this work?

In my "I'm not sure of myself as an author" mode, I said, "I have a list of fifty literary journals, and I am considering sending my essay to twenty or more."

"Where do you find these journals?" he asked. "Are they available in New York?"

"The public library and the university libraries," I told him. "And I have a research assistant who reviews literary journals to see if my work fits with what they publish."

Michael was lively and talked fast; he seemed focused, determined, and successful. It turned out that he was a literary agent. He told me he and his wife lived in San Francisco and coproduced the annual San Francisco Writers Conference. He also told me about a great little apartment to rent a few blocks away. Later I Googled him and found out that he was a published author of books on how to write a book proposal and how to find an agent.

After close to a half-hour conversation, I said, "This all started with you saying, 'Bless you.'"

As he put on his coat and gathered up his *New York Times*, we said our good-byes, and he offered me his card. "Please call me," he said. "We are always interested in nonfiction work."

I accepted his card with gratitude.

As he turned toward the door, he said, "And what you are doing is just what you should be doing."

My husband and I live in Kensington, a small village north of Berkeley and my home since 1980. I have a separate room where I do my writing. I start between eight and nine in the morning. My routine begins with grinding Peet's coffee beans and brewing my decaf Americano in our espresso machine, for which we paid five dollars at an estate sale. I prefer a bare minimum of talk—a "Good morning," and "How did you sleep?" A kiss and a hug from my husband, and then I'm off to work.

From the kitchen, I walk down thirteen steps, turn left, and head down the hall past the laundry room, sauna, and bathroom to unlock my study. Entering, I feel welcomed by my room with knotty pine paneling and a large, south-facing window that gets the morning sun as it travels west. My eye catches the large charcoal painting I did of an African woman who modeled for a drawing class I took at Chicago's Art Institute in 1996; then a smaller, framed watercolor painting I did as I sat in a café in Paris on a rainy day last March.

I set my banana and my mug, which reads "You Can't Make This Stuff Up," on a separate table to the left of my desk, far enough away that I can't spill coffee on my computer. As I sit at my desk and open my computer, I exhale and I look up at the wall, which is covered from eye-level to the ceiling in black-and-white photographs I shot in Central Park in January 2009 in the snow, plus some other framed photos of my family. The one that makes me smile is of my daughter and her husband on their wedding day, radiating happiness. I won't reappear upstairs until I am hungry for breakfast around ten thirty or so.

Alone in my study, I feel such satisfaction. It is a place where I bring my hopes and joys as a writer, but also where I struggle with doubts and frustrations. I struggle to be deeply truthful, what Dorothy Allison refers to as being "naked on the page." Dorothy was the mother of our tribe of twelve writers at a Tomales Bay five-day workshop on a narrow inlet on the Pacific Ocean in Northern California in the fall of 2011. She demanded that we be naked on the page in our writings.

On my drive home from that workshop, I stopped at Point Reyes Regional Park and walked the Bear Valley Trail to the Arch, an eight-mile hike. I let my thoughts roam free, and as I did, I discovered the connection between being naked on the page and being more honest with my husband.

If I could not tell him my desires and needs and feelings, regardless of whether the truth might hurt him, how could I be honest in my writing? How could I dig down deep about my own fears, disappointments, and sadness? But it was about more than being honest with my husband; it was about my own fear of facing myself. Ursula, a wise, older friend, told me in 1993 that she saw sadness in my eyes. At the time, I proclaimed that the sadness I was carrying came from the work I was doing interviewing women about their HIV status. That was true. Each interview made me aware of how much the women with HIV/AIDS carried the burden of whom they could and could not to disclose to. The pain of being stigmatized was evident in these women.

The evening after I arrived home from the workshop, I said to my husband, "I have something I want to say to you. As a writer, I am selfish. I know that. I am selfish about wanting to be alone to write. I am selfish when I wake in the morning and head to my study. My writing takes a high priority in my life. The only way I can write is by being alone.

"Along with this isolation, I need other writers and artists who understand the way I work. And I have gathered women writers and our daughter and son-in-law as my supporters. And I know you want to be one of those, but you are not. And probably you will never be that for me. I know you realize that when you ask questions, and I roll my eyes or avoid looking at you. My expression probably tells you how irritated and impatient I am. Like the time I returned from my first writers' conference that I attended to explore the world of nonfiction publishing. When you picked me up at the airport you asked me, 'Did you learn to write?' And I said, 'You learn to write by writing.'"

It was important to me to let Ken know what I needed as a writer.

I looked into my husband's eyes. "You will never be one of those people, and that's okay. So you don't have to ask me questions about my writing."

We stood there looking at each other for a while. Nothing more was said.

For me it felt good to be honest and forthright, but I also wondered if I had been unkind. That night at dinner, sitting across from each other at the round oak table in our kitchen and eating my homemade chicken enchiladas, I found our conversation was less guarded and more open. I asked him if I had been too harsh in my comments.

"No," he said. "It was clear." His words were said in kindness.

I felt that he had heard me. I had succeeded in telling my truth and speaking with honesty and integrity. For now, this was a good start.

The next morning, I went to my study, an action that had become just as much a habit as brushing my teeth. Now I had to get naked on the page. Though challenging for me, I have had incremental steps of success.

Within weeks of my conversation with my husband, I found myself at dinner with a writer friend at a Chinese restaurant. As we lingered over our wine, we took turns reading our fortunes. I opened my fortune cookie and read to her, "Don't be pushed by your problems. Be led by your dreams."

As I sit down to write, I feel supported by Ken. He honors my request by knocking on my study door and waiting for a response as opposed to just coming in, and for this I am grateful.

Romance on an
Alaskan Cruise

In 2008, with the stock market taking it's biggest loss since 1929, my husband, Ken, and I decided to go on his long-desired Alaskan cruise. Perhaps it was not the smartest economic decision. It could be called "living on the edge," which apparently our nation was modeling.

The thirty-one-year-old captain was navigating Alaska's eastern Inside Passage heading to Brother's Island in the Frederick Sound. Our ship of about sixty passengers was marketed as "a personal and up-close experience" for adventure. A casual atmosphere had developed among the passengers and crew. The captain, who preferred to be called Mark, had invited people to visit him on the bridge to trade stories or ask questions. The expedition leaders, chef, and other staff regularly joined us in the dining room to get their meals, though they ate elsewhere.

"Tucker, that's your name, isn't it?" I asked.

"Yes," he said, looking at me, his black marble eyes seeming to hold delight at being called by name.

Tucker was a crew member I had observed assisting passengers into kayaks and steering the Zodiacs used for our shore excursions. We were at the toaster section against the wall in the functional dining room, sun streaming through high windows of our ship, aptly named *The Adventurer*. The room was buzzing with hungry voyagers lined up at the steam table helping themselves to breakfast. The aromas of toast, sausage, and coffee woke up my enthusiasm for hiking a bear trail, though my reasonable self considered this insane, given my deep-seated fear of bears. I had only seen a bear once, at Nevada Falls in Yosemite. He had lumbered to the water's edge, scooped up a fish, ate it, and left me gaping at the sight, my heart doing double time. It was enough bear sighting for me to last a lifetime.

Earlier in the cruise, I was captivated by Tucker's good looks. His face was classic. Sharp angular jaw, pointed nose, skin the color of milk chocolate, in striking contrast to his jet-black hair, neatly trimmed close to his oval-shaped head. Tucker's thin-lined beard framed his unblemished face as if the master painter, Van Dyck, had designed him.

Tucker was using metal tongs to retrieve his English muffin from the toaster.

"That's risky," I said.

He looked at me like a child being caught doing something wrong. Realizing I might have sounded more aggressive than I meant to, I quickly changed the subject. With my library voice I inquired, "What nationality are you?"

"What nationality do you think I am?" he said shyly, looking at me, and then quickly turning back to the toaster. "People often ask me, and I'm curious what you think."

"Well, I'm Italian, so I want you to be Italian," I replied. We laughed, enjoying the illusion of intimacy.

"I'm Iranian and Irish," he said.

"Which parent is which?" I questioned.

"My father was Iranian, and my mother was Irish." He smiled, with a timid, sleepy-eyed look. I read it as an "I hope you like me" look.

I thought that was the end of our casual conversation. And I would have been happy to have shared our interlude and shown my admiration for his good looks and demeanor. But then he added, "I didn't know my parents. I was adopted."

Now I didn't know what to say to that. Moments before, probably sometime after "Good morning," I had said, "You have such a classic face, it makes me want to draw you. That may sound like a come-on, but I am an amateur painter." Or did I say *artist*? How foolish of me. Honestly, what a dumb thing to say. He was probably in his early twenties and I in my early seventies.

What a fantasy to meet such a handsome young man, early in his life, who appeared not to be arrogant but seemed unaware of his good looks. He was well mannered and unassuming. As a crew member on this cruise, he was no doubt trained to be nice to the passengers. But in my head, as in a dream, I felt a romance developing. What if I were younger? What if crew and passengers comingled after hours? What if a secret romp in a secluded part of the ship were possible? What if we were caught? What if I got pregnant? I let my fantasy run wild.

When I was in my early twenties, I was so stupidly naive about men. I mean, looking back, I was inexperienced in heterosexual relationships. What little we were taught in high school by our gym teacher, Miss Shaffer, a single woman, consisted of a few impersonal anatomical line drawings, and mostly had to do with getting pregnant or not. One memorable fact was, "You can't get pregnant from a toilet seat."

I don't recall any instructions from my parents about "the birds and the bees," the euphemism for sex instruction in the 1950s. Sex was a topic even my best girlfriends didn't discuss, nor my two older sisters. I later learned one sister agreed with me and said she knew as little as I did. My older sister said our parents never told her anything, but she found a book on the lower shelf of a glassed-in bookcase in our home that she read in secret. She recalled saying to her best friend, "I know everything about sex," but confessed to me that she really knew nothing. How we were to learn about men was a mystery to be solved without any tools except to be a good girl as opposed to a bad one.

I had gone steady in high school twice, once in my junior year with Tom, and then with Del in my senior year. There were other more casual dates, but all were with gentlemen who never pushed beyond first base. "Gentleman" was the word that defined a man who respected women. My parents expected that when I went on a date, the gentleman would come into my home to meet them, neatly dressed, clean-shaven, and with shoes polished. He would open the car door for me, pay for the movie or the high school dance, hold my arm as we walked, and have no expectation of sexual payback. There was a cultural understanding that it was the woman who determined how far the man could go, meaning a kiss, a feel, or more.

There was one exception in my experience. I was a junior in high school when I accepted an offer of a ride home from the head cheerleader of the opposing school after a football game. He was not a gentleman, but rather a rogue, a despicable, contemptible young man. He pushed beyond first base, to my surprise going straight for third, but I escaped before he scored. Thanks to my dad's advice, we were parked in my own long driveway. Dad had told me I could not park with my dates any place other than our driveway. He said it wasn't safe in other areas of our small town. At the time I had no idea what he meant by "not safe." After the cheerleader, I had a better idea. I trusted and respected my dad.

I led a sheltered life where boys were concerned. I was "Daddy's little girl," being the third daughter in the birth order of four, with a baby brother. In high school, when a boy called me up for a date, I would say, "I have to ask my parents." While the boy was on the phone with the receiver hanging from the wall, I would walk from the kitchen into the living room to ask my parents and wait while Mom and Dad began a dialog about his parents. Had Mom gone to school with his mother? Did Dad know his father from work? Had Dad played baseball with his father, or was it his brother? I would eventually say, "Well can I go out with him or not? He's waiting on the phone."

After high school, I felt left behind as I grudgingly went to the local junior college while my friends ventured into the world beyond our town to take their places at four-year schools.

The year I entered junior college science became paramount in education as a reaction to the Soviet Union's launching of Sputnik. The race was on to put a man in space. That suited me. I was a serious student. I did nothing but study and work to make money with a plan to leave for university after graduation. Dating was something I was too busy to consider. Anyway, most of the best guys had left for college.

My maiden voyage away from home was a summer waitress job after I graduated from junior college and before leaving for university. Once again, Mom was reluctant to let me go. The job was at Hoberg's, a family resort, two and a half hours north of our home in Lake County. She called the resort the "pit of sin." But with my father's support, and the fact that my mother's relatives lived close by the resor

For all my naivety about romantic relationships, I left home after that summer for an undergraduate degree at UC San Francisco, a predominately male university. I was one of eighteen female dental hygiene students taking lecture courses with one hundred freshman male dental students. They were all older than I, some having had military service, all having completed an undergraduate degree.

I was the only woman on the dental school student council. While waiting for the dean to join us, I blushed at the casual conversation the three male members were having about shaving. I know, it's hard to believe that a conversation about shaving would make a twenty-year-old blush. It is painful for me to remember.

In another dental school episode, I was such a simpleton that I was not initially aware when Stan, a third-year dental student whom I thought of as a friend, was getting sexually aroused from rubbing his leg against mine at a communal table for lunch in the crowded campus cafeteria. He laughed at me when I became conscious of his lecherous smile. I abruptly got up and walked away, red-faced, as he was laughing.

When or how did I gain some wisdom and judgment about men? I can tell you, it was long in developing. I have very fond memories of my introduction to romantic relationships in high school and when I went away to college. Then taking my academic degree and my dental hygiene license to Hawaii for my first job as public health dental hygienist, I left behind a boyfriend, a doctoral student in pharmacology, and before him, an orthodontic student. Both gentlemen. So I was unprepared for the attorney I met and dated in Hawaii. He was older by seven years, a wolf in sheep's clothing. We mutually ended the relationship when I returned after a year to a job as assistant professor teaching at UC San Francisco in the dental hygiene department.

My education about men came far too slowly to prevent my most disagreeable relationship. It was a year after the attorney that I met the dentist from the Midwest, while attending a national dental conference in Miami with my former college roommate Carol. He was divorced, slightly bald, with a bulging stomach, and wore glasses. He was funny, flattering, and fibbing. I'll call him "the Horse's Patoot." During our long-distance courtship, we flew back and forth. I introduced him to my family. He introduced me to his two young daughters. We talked of marriage. He bought me a designer engagement ring. This was during the social revolution known as the "Summer of Love." My philosophy was the opposite of this counterculture known for "free love" with "hippies" challenging the status quo with drug use and frequent sex. I wanted no part of the movement. But I felt burdened by the broad assumption that any single woman was eager for sex. The long-distance fiancé was my shield against unwanted advances. When my women friends pointed out some of his weaker characteristics, I was defensive and stood up for him. My family was cordial toward him, neither enthused nor critical about our engagement. This shield, though comforting, blinded me to clues that he was not telling me the truth.

When we began making plans for our wedding, he said, "I want to marry you as soon as possible, you know that. But I think for my girls' sake, we should wait until they're older.

Of course I believed him. I always believed him. "How long do you think that would be?" I asked.

"Well, a year, maybe two," he said. "But let's not talk about that. I have been waiting to take you to this special restaurant. It's romantic with a violinist who plays songs like 'La Vie en Rose.' We could drink champagne and stay out late and. . . ."

He had that look of love. And I was in love and stupid enough not to acknowledge his sleight of hand in changing the subject of wedding plans.

Months later, our telephone conversations still always seemed to end with Horse's Patoot's excuses for postponing the wedding. The themes were his family, the girls' recitals or graduation, and his work, how hard it would be to take time off from his patients. As time went on, it became clear my family and friends were not enthused about Horse's Patoot, and it wore on me. I began asking myself questions. Did I really want to live in a manufacturing town that was nothing like San Francisco? Was I serious about giving up my career to become a dentist's wife? And we haven't ever talked religion or politics. For all I knew he was a Republican!

As I traveled less often to the Midwest to visit him and saw him mostly in San Francisco, where fewer of my friends joined us for the evening, I began to take stock. In a particularly heated telephone argument when I let him know I was tired of waiting, Horse's Patoot came clean. He couldn't set the wedding date because he was married. He was still living with his wife, but he had seen an attorney; no, he hadn't told his wife, but they hadn't slept together, blah, blah, blah.

Bastard! I thought, but I was too polite to push back. He was worse than a horse's patoot. For all my belief that I was becoming an independent woman, *I* felt like the horse's ass. Why hadn't I suspected anything?

I didn't start out with this in mind. Though he betrayed me, I went right to the feeling that it was my fault. I was the "other" woman. And that was shameful in my eyes.

The irony is that my best friend, Carol, knew all along that the patoot was not divorced. When I asked her why she hadn't told me, she said "I didn't want to interfere." I told her that had been a mistake, and she could have saved me a lot of heartache.

He called me once after that, while I was in the bathtub, a vulnerable place to be, even long distance. As soon as I heard his voice I yelled, "Don't ever call me again!" and slammed down the receiver.

As I look back, I was disappointed in myself as I buried that hurtful relationship without the guts to call him out for what he was. But moving forward, I embraced my single career-woman status, determined not to marry anytime soon.

When I told my parents the engagement was off, my mom hugged me and said she was sorry that the relationship did not work out. Dad didn't say much. I couldn't bring myself to confess the truth to them, and we never spoke about it again. To my parents' dismay, though, I was twenty-five, unmarried, and with no immediate prospects. My mother stopped asking me when I was going to get married. I believe she thought I was an old maid, or maybe a loose woman since I lived in my own apartment. I don't know which label was worse. I no longer lived in the small town where I had grown up, and perhaps the old wives' tale of the wanton woman who left her hometown for the big city had landed on me.

It was shortly after that when Ken, the lifeguard from Hoberg's, called me for a date after six years.

When I saw Tucker again, we only exchanged pleasantries. I did make a sketch of him from the upper deck, while watching him swab the decks below. I knew so little about him. But his kindness was evident, not just with me, but with everyone on board. His beauty and gentleness remain in my memory.

As my husband and I disembarked after shaking hands with the line of staff, ending with the captain, I was brought back to reality. I turned to my husband of forty-six years and wondered, *Was Tucker the current version of Lifeguard Ken? Was my fantasy romance on our Alaskan cruise my yearning for our youthful selves? Could we recapture the romance we'd had that first summer we met?* As I was pondering this, Ken offered his arm, and we stepped off the plank onto solid ground.

To Love One Another Till

As my husband and I journey toward our fiftieth anniversary, three years away, I am watching his memory decline. A couple of years ago, Ken was diagnosed with mild cognitive impairment, and it's quickly gotten worse. Is this to be the most challenging part of our marriage? Is this to be the ultimate test or trial of our promise to love one another till. . . ?

It is not so much the lost keys, the forgotten appointment, or the misplaced car. This I can help him with. Like a detective, I ask questions and make deductions. I've learned ways to help prevent a missed appointment, for example, or a function where he's been invited to give a talk. I keep his appointments and engagements in my calendar, as well as in his. And we check in daily about what is on his schedule for the day.

What is more difficult and at times frightening is Ken's total loss of interactions we have had, be it a date, a conversation, or a decision. Recently we made a date to go for a walk, for instance, but he was at a café reading, part of his regular routine, and did not show up at all, nor did he call. Frequently, he will ask me the same question three or four times, often within a few minutes. "What time are we going to the movies?" "What time are our friends picking us up for dinner?" Out of the blue one morning, he said he was going to have lab work done for a routine cardiology appointment. I have been attending his cardiology appointments since the beginning of his declining memory, and I record the nurse's report as well as the subsequent appointments. Ken tells me how much he appreciates my presence.

So when he informed me he was going for his lab work, I had to remind him that the appointment was two months away. The instructions written on the lab prescription required that the work be done the week of the appointment. You'd think that I would get used to his declining memory and behavior, but it stuns me every time.

One of the first indications of his memory declining was when he called one day to say he could not find his car. He was returning from a lecture series at a seminary close to the UC Berkeley campus. As an alumnus, he knows this area well. He regularly attends athletic events on the campus. Previously we'd discussed the idea of him writing down the street and the cross street upon parking the car. He had done this, but even so, he'd looked for quite a while before he called me. In the process, he'd become confused. I went to where he was and found the car based on his note. Besides being frustrated, Ken was embarrassed and upset with himself. I was sad for him and encouraged him to be gentler with himself. I considered trying to add something humorous but decided it was perhaps not the best strategy at this moment.

I admire that Ken does not hide his aging or his declining memory. I have heard him on the telephone and in person as he openly admits, "My memory is not what it used to be, so please let me write down what you are telling me." I've learned, however, that despite this strategy, he might not remember where he wrote the information. On his own initiative, Ken has begun carrying a small leather folder that contains a pen and paper, which has eased some of this problem. At his best, he will make a point of writing commitments in his pocket paper calendar. He also keeps a larger paper calendar at his desk at home in his office space. He uses a computer for emails, searching websites, and preparing sermons but has not moved to an electronic calendar that would be backed up to his computer. This could have the advantage of not losing information if the paper version is misplaced, something that has happened more times than I care to document.

My husband's losing his keys, wallet, credit card, calendar, or car is more frustrating for him than it is for me, though at times it gets me too. It seems to me that his lack of resiliency undermines him; by that I mean his ability to bounce back, shrug it off. Certainly I have misplaced things. Don't we all? The difference is that I can retrace my steps and recall where and when I last had the item, something that is not available to him as easily, and sometimes not at all.

Ken is completely capable of maintaining his daily functions, and he has not completely retired. He works half-time as a ministerial sabbatical leave replacement for a small church. Though recently he said this might be the last church he will serve. The reason, he said, was his memory loss.

We can both manage his declining memory, and yet I'm often surprised by his diminished ability at times to reason and think rationally. In October 2014, we were vacationing in a small cottage by the beach with our daughter. Though the sun was shining, the cool air and wind made it uncomfortable to be sitting outside for very long. On this particular Sunday, we were all together in the one large area that included the kitchen, living room, and a large TV. Ken's Sunday routine after attending church and eating lunch was to watch televised sports with the volume turned up. With the three of us in the cottage, I asked if he could please reduce his TV watching to two hours rather than his usual four. His immediate response was anger toward me, saying that I had belittled him in front of our daughter. This behavior was atypical; he seldom got mad at me and would apologize later. He would not be consoled. His ability to be reasonable seemed to have vanished. Later that day, our daughter talked to him in private. She said, "What Mom said was not belittling. It seemed appropriate given the circumstances." Ordinarily he would listen with respect and engage in meaningful conversation. But in this instance Ken was as immoveable as the rock of Gibraltar. His response to her was startling, we were both surprised by his aggressive behavior.

It is this surprising response to a reasonable situation that leaves me feeling that I am living with a child, not my husband. This saddens and frustrates me and makes life unpredictable.

I have watched Ken go from a marathon runner in his mid-forties to running a half-marathon in his early seventies, and eventually giving up jogging altogether. He does regularly work out on an elliptical bike that is parked in our family room.

I have watched him go from being a good dresser to an old man wearing sloppy pants and shirts with food stains over his pregnant-looking stomach. A particularly startling public example of his appearance was when he, along with six other ministers, some older and some younger, were asked to speak for five minutes at a seventy-fifth anniversary celebration of Orinda Community Church. They had all served this church at different times over the years. His appearance was startling to me even though I'd left the house with him. I was embarrassed now that I saw him as others must see him, such a far fall from his former self. As the other six ministers were dressed in suits and ties, Ken wore ill-fitting wash pants and a black turtleneck with an athletic insignia that peeked out from the right side of his rayon navy blazer. It looked as if his clothes had come from a bag on its way to the second-hand store.

Later after dinner, I said to Ken, "Why don't we go through your wardrobe, and you try on everything, and what is worn out or has stains or doesn't cover you, it goes out. It took over an hour and a half with him trying on every shirt, sweater, pants, and suit. Together we eliminated what no longer fit or looked good on him. He was in a playful mood, and we were having fun. We didn't finish till eight thirty, but I had an idea. "Now let's go to the REI store and buy you some new clothes.

Ken raised his eyebrows and said, "Now?" Are they still open?"

"Oh, yes," I said. He was game, and we purchased some good-looking and well-fitting clothes in grays, blacks, and dark greens. He had the wide-eyed expression of an angelfish when the cashier tallied our purchases. But on this night, he was delighted with the attention and the results. When dressed well, he reminds me of Paul Newman.

After this experience, I realized that yet another of my responsibilities was going to be making sure he was well dressed.

It was even more difficult to watch Ken speak, the second of the seven men and one woman ministers to deliver their remembrances about their ministry at this church. He had written a script and practiced it the previous night and in the early morning before we left for the event. He is a good public speaker, but during the service, he went off script and began rambling. Ken talked more about himself, focusing on his telephone job interview and how he was freezing in Scotland at the time, when it was noted by an interview committee member how hot it was in Orinda. Ken went on about organizing a youth trip to an orphanage, focusing more on himself than the purpose of the trip; how he drove a sick youth to Tijuana to the doctor, only to return to find the majority of the group was sick, and the toilets were jammed. He talked for twenty minutes.

The officiating minister who had planned the event was sitting in the chancel behind the line of ministers waiting for their turn to speak. Somewhere about ten minutes past Ken's allotted five minutes, the officiating minister stood up. He walked to the altar, fussed with something, and walked back to his seat. I'm not sure Ken was aware of his movement as he continued his rambling. Ken was usually well prepared and conscious of the time.

At the end of the service my friend turned to me and said, sympathetically "Do you think you will say something to Ken?" I thought for a moment, then said, "I will see what he says about his speech, to determine if he is self-aware."

After an extended celebratory lunch, we were in our car driving home. I asked him what he thought of the celebration. "I think it went well," he said, "but I thought the service could have been shorter." I chose not to comment. Then he asked, "What did you think?"

"I thought Ray and John both did a wonderful job of giving the congregation and the staff credit, by naming individuals, for the social justice issues that they had helped facilitate," I said. "And I enjoyed Ray's brief history about the church members and his struggling with the county to achieve rezoning of the church property in order to build senior housing." I was hoping by inference that he would realize his more lengthy, self-centered remarks were off point and inappropriate. But he seemed unaware, or perhaps aware but not wanting to admit it or talk about it.

We are aging at a different rate. Now I always hold on to the handrail and look at the steps as I descend stairs, not taking my eyes off the last step in particular. It is a known fact that it is the last step that can do a person in. It means more trips up and down the stairs to my study and laundry room in order to have one hand on the rail to prevent a fall. My other hand holds onto my coffee, or computer, or laundry basket.

That's multiple trips, but worth the time and the added exercise to stay safe in a two-story home. I still walk three times a week, but at a slower pace and with walking poles. My right knee talks to me at times due to a skiing accident I had in my mid-twenties.

Today I depend on my computer and cell phone where I have my contacts and photos to assist me, but I also think most people rely on these devices as a memory aid. And so far, I have not lost either. The last thing about my aging is that I have never been good with remembering names, so I can't lose that skill. It has never been with me. What I fear losing most is my independence. I am, in fact, watching it being chipped away already, as Ken becomes more dependent on me. My fear is that as time passes, I will have less and less of my life. Will I have time to myself to write, to see my family and friends, and to travel? As I hold tight to my lifestyle, increasingly there is a pattern of my giving and his taking, with little reciprocity. And at times I not only fear losing my lifestyle, but I get tired of giving.

There are gestures that I love about my husband and our relationship. I love that he kisses me good morning and good night. I love that he takes out the garbage, does the grocery shopping, and cleans the dishes after dinner. I love that he knocks on my study door and waits for a "Come in" before entering. I love that he seldom disturbs me when I am writing in my study. I love that he accepts, if not understanding, that I do not like to talk much in the mornings. I love that we still watch *Masterpiece Theatre* on Sundays and have for over fifty years, since the original series of *Upstairs, Downstairs* aired in 1974.

I love that I still cut Ken's hair and have since we were engaged and writing our wedding vows as he sat on a kitchen stool in my parents' home in 1968. I love that he cried at my graduation in 1992 when I was called by name to the stage and was hooded by Dr. Adele Clarke, who announced my dissertation title. Descending the steps, I heard the applause as I exuberantly raised my arms in joy. When the ceremony was over, I was surprised at Ken's tears. Upon reflection, it seemed to me that this public recognition of me helped him acknowledge my work.

If I could change anything, I would want Ken to laugh at my jokes. I would want him to be proud of my volunteer work and not be disdainful and fake interest or be plain uninterested with eyes rolling in boredom or looking away as I speak. I would want him to share more joy and be more enthusiastic about living and talk less about death. He seems to have frequent "death reports," a term that our family now uses to describe his recurring conversations on death and dying. And I would enjoy him having a less ponderous style of speech.

But I also think about the future, and I'm hopeful. At times I luxuriate in thinking about our fiftieth wedding anniversary celebration. I envision a large gathering of family and friends for a weekend at Hoberg's Resort, where Ken and I met. In my more realistic frame of mind, and when I step back and contemplate our life together, I realize the gradual loss is Ken, as his memory diminishes. And if I don't precede him in death, I know Ken's inevitable death will be the biggest loss. And then will I regret my tight grasp on my own independence? Only time will tell.

Why I Stay

The short answer to why I stay married is that I never contemplated leaving.

My family tradition was, "You make your bed, you lie in it." I suppose our ancestors chose their spouse very carefully, and once married, stayed married and lived up to the tradition. There would have been other reasons, too, of course, like financial security, protection from danger, and the difficulties of unmarried women to be assimilated into a community.

There were only two divorces in my immediate family, a half-century apart. So it was an unusual event. I believed that marriage was a sacrament, even though I was no longer a practicing Catholic and was married to a Protestant minister. My early catechism as well as selected Catholic doctrine stuck with me.

I remember clearly a few weeks before our wedding in 1968, Ken sitting on a high stool next to the yellow wall phone in my parents' kitchen as I cut his hair. We talked through what we wanted to promise as we wrote our vows. We promised a lot, including lifelong companionship, to be loving spouses, and our bond of love. In our wedding we vowed to love one another in "our happy and sad times, during good or bad health, and in whatever circumstances our union leads us."

We promised to love each other forever.

I still recall that I felt the word *forever* was hard to believe in, even to say. And now, in retrospect, I am not sure I did believe in forever, even on my wedding day.

Looking back over fifty years of marriage and pondering why I stay, there is a simple truth. I am married to a nice person. A characteristic of our marriage is kindness, though we've had our difficult times. The first four years of marriage, we had arguments about his drinking with no resolution. It was a turning point in our marriage when Ken recognized that he was an alcoholic and started going to Alcoholics Anonymous meetings, which he continues to attend with forty-three years of sobriety. He is comfortable around other people's drinking, including my own. His sobriety, I know, is one step at a time. I am proud of Ken for his sobriety. I have faith in him to continue to be sober, and I am extremely grateful to him.

There was only one argument where things got physical, and I'm not proud of the fact that I was the aggressor. One night, early in our marriage. as we were getting ready for bed, we were having an argument that was going nowhere, over what I don't remember. But I threw his shoe at him, though it missed and hit the ceiling. Nevertheless, I regretted my outburst terribly and instantly because it was not in my character to resort to violence. I grew up in a home where my parents would argue, at times loud enough for us children to hear, but there was never any physical violence. It was my bad luck and aim that the shoe left a mark on the ceiling that served as a constant reminder to me of my poor behavior, as it was the last thing I saw before I closed my eyes at night. I never again threw anything.

In addition to being kind, Ken has been a financial stabilizer. He has worked steadily and enjoyed his work enormously. There are few people I know who are as well suited to their work as he is. I have worked steadily over the years, other than unpaid leaves while birthing and mothering our daughter, as there was no family or maternity leave in 1973. I also needed Ken's financial support when I was a full-time graduate student in 1989 through 1992. I was awarded a paid sabbatical, a scholarship, plus fellowships and grants during that time, but not equivalent to my salary when I took a leave without pay.

Ken and I share compatible values about how we spend our money. Saving and investing funds was something we had to work on in our marriage. Early on Ken had to be convinced by my stockbroker that investing money in the market was important. Ken and I have not regretted this use of our money.

We did regret the loss of funds we invested outside our stockbroker, because the person in charge of the limited partnership investment was guilty of illegal actions, and we lost our entire investment. I learned to be more assertive about our money. And I was not above fault-finding and blaming my husband since he had learned about this investment and been more enthused about it.

However, another investment outside our stockbroker that Ken initiated paid off in an unexpected way. We were shocked and pleased with our windfall. It not only allowed us to recoup the previous loss, but we were in complete agreement when we said simultaneously, "Let's buy our home." Being in harmony, as in that case, has made our relationship easier and more pleasant.

Our daughter has had a steady father in Ken, who from the beginning was excited and happy to be called "Daddy." Even though he had told me when I was pregnant that he would not be able to get up in the middle of the night because he needed his sleep for work, when she first cried in the night, hungry for her feeding, he was the first one up to change her and bring her to me in bed.

From her dad, our daughter learned that she could take risks. As a young child, she wanted to climb up the huge pine tree in our front yard that was taller than our roofline. I had to go into the house because I could not watch for fear of her falling.

One time she climbed high up in a pine tree, a story that Ken recounted to me later. "Daddy, I can't get down," she'd said.

"Sure you can," Ken said. "I'm here to talk you down." He climbed up as far as he could but wasn't able reach her, as the spaces between branches were too small for him. Ken talked her through it, and she got down, a little shaken but proud of herself.

There were other physical adventures between the two of them, like rafting and hiking, sometimes scary. I believe their relationship helped make her a risk-taker, a quality that has helped make her the strong woman she is today.

In retrospect, our first few years of marriage were both fun-filled and frustrating for me. There are two incidents that stand out that served as a foundation for my understanding of what it would be like to be married to Ken. The day of our wedding, I began to get a glimmer that later turned into a realization that I had fallen in love with and married a man who put his work before me. The first words he said to me as my husband in the narthex of the church, as we were leaving the sanctuary to accompanying applause, was, "I thought the service was too long. Chauncey spoke too long."

I was hoping for, "You look so beautiful. I love you so much." I was stunned speechless. It wasn't the time nor the place to tell him how hurt I was. So I swallowed my disappointment and tried not to think about it as I put on my "public" face to greet our guests in the receiving line in the fellowship hall.

The second week of our marriage, I learned the honeymoon was over. We were both back to our full-time jobs when one night he told me he was going out for dinner that evening with a group of ministers. The group included some of our mutual friends, but he said it wouldn't be appropriate to bring me, and that he would probably be out late.

Looking back, I see that was certainly reasonable. But I was hurt that he was going out within the first few days of our married life at home. To me, being in our first home that week was particularly special, after a wonderful honeymoon.

When Ken left to go to dinner, I realized that I was in a marriage where I would have to take care of myself. I knew that I would need a separate life that would involve my own career. However, it was a mystery to me how Ken would care for my emotional needs. This aspect of our marriage could not be as easily solved as maintaining my identity in a career. I figured out that I would need to learn, and quickly, how to share in a rational way what was on my mind and to talk about my feelings. I had to erase from my mind the crazy notion that, "If he loved me, he would know . . ." In the larger sense, I knew I was thrilled to be his wife; however, that night the afterglow of wedding and honeymoon was looking as fragile as a spider's web in a gust of wind.

Emotionally, I had hoped for continued respect and love. If the truth be told, I also wanted adoration. But I realized the night of the dinner with his fellow ministers that I would come second to his work. This awareness was never a reason to leave, but it was a defining moment for me as his wife. It forced me to see the reality that I would have to continue to be self-sufficient, just as I had been prior to marriage. I knew I had the resources for that, even though it was not what I had expected. That night I slept on the couch, cried into my pillow, and pretended to be asleep when he came home.

Another reason Ken and I work is because we've been good at compromise. The most treasured and compassionate thing that Ken did for me happened five years after our daughter was born, ten years into our marriage. I wanted to have a second child, and Ken was not interested. We had discussed this many times. His usual reasoning was that another child would take away from the time he had for parenting the daughter we had. He expressed that he would have to divide his time between a baby and our daughter, basically implying that there was a limited amount of time to commit to parenting. Was this reasonable? Perhaps, but I felt hurt and disappointed. This cloud of disagreement lasted for many months. Finally he said to me, "I don't want to have another child, but you mean more to me than my not wanting another, so I am willing to commit to your desire."

I loved him for coming around to this, for doing this for me, for putting aside his own needs. But then with each month that I got my period, I felt let down and sad. As the months passed, I tried to keep my hopes up. But as months began to close into a year, the sadness became mixed, and hope was replaced with relief. I feared for the potential risks of pregnancy and birth at age thirty-eight. By the standards of the seventies, I had been old at thirty-two when I had our daughter.

Eventually, I came to redefine three as a family, and I was satisfied. I reveled in the continuing development of an especially close relationship with my daughter. I came to realize in this one daughter, I had all the children I needed.

Now that Ken and I have been married for fifty years, I ask myself, *What makes our marriage work and survive? Is it love, kindness, peacefulness, security, shared parenting?* It is some of these characteristics, yes. It's also our shared history of decisions, experiences, and compromises.

We jointly decided that since we had one child, we would parent as if she were our second or third child. We resolved to treat her as a full member of our family, encouraging her thoughts and ideas. At the dinner table, we tried not to interrupt one another, including her. We listened when she spoke and nurtured her contributions. We promised to not spoil her. We supported her choices of courses in middle and high school, as well as her choice of college. It was easy to agree on her curfew when she suggested eleven o'clock. We were surprised when, during her senior year, she told us she was auditioning for Alvin Ailey's summer intensive dance program in New York City. When she was accepted, Ken and I both applauded her success, and he in turn supported my decision to go to New York to be chaperone while doing research for my dissertation.

Ken and I have both achieved satisfaction and success in our work lives. However, we are still learning how to rejoice in each other's separate worlds. The feminist movement helped me strive for equality that challenged our marriage.

Over the years, we have reassigned division of domestic labor, helped along by necessity, as I was out of the home more during graduate school and starting a new career after our daughter went to college. Ken's sabbatical experience of living in a monastic community where everyone had daily chores influenced his attitude toward domestic labor. He came home from his experience and said he would do kitchen clean-up after dinner. Out of necessity, he eventually laundered his own clothes. This supported my change of lifestyle and helped our marriage. I gained more respect for him for sharing domestic responsibilities, while trying hard to let go of my attitude toward house-proud standards.

Time apart in our marriage has been essential for me, and perhaps for us. Our separations have been for career-oriented reasons, like Ken's sabbatical leave in Montreal, or my fellowship

at the University of Illinois at Chicago for a semester where I
lived doing research.

Over the years, my research has allowed me to travel to
New York frequently for data collection, where I also visited
our daughter and son-in-law. I have traveled more often
than Ken for my work, giving presentations at conferences
in Barcelona, Washington, DC, Paris, and Montreal. These
times apart were exciting, and an opportunity to have my work
shared with other scientists working in similar fields of study.
I appreciate being able to focus only on my work and being
responsible for my needs only.

When Ken resigned from the church he had served for
twenty-three years, he expected to do interim ministry close to
home, but that did not happen. For a period of some months,
we agreed, with advice from our financial advisor, to borrow
money from Ken's life insurance to be used to replace a portion
of his salary. After perhaps six months when there were no
available interim positions close to home, and with my encouragement to look farther afield, Ken served a church where he
lived in Southern California for eighteen months. We would
visit each other as time and need permitted. It was not unlike
dating, flying back and forth for time together. This was not
without its problems, as his days off did not coincide with
mine. When I visited him on the weekends, it was his busiest
time. There was no easy solution, but we compromised and
made the best of it.

I am proud of us. Over the course of our fifty-one years,
we have allowed a freedom in our marriage that encourages
both of us to continue to grow. I am grateful that Ken has
been willing and able to change with the social evolution and
to adapt to the encompassing demands of equality for women
in work and in family. Many men of his generation might not
have been able or willing to adapt. Ken has adjusted to the
ways in which my feminist value of equality has redesigned

our domestic and professional lives. I am proud of our shared history of our marriage, parenting, and our inherited families, with years of holiday celebrations, and the marriages, births, and deaths, several of which my husband has officiated as the family pastor.

There was one occasion he did not officiate. Our daughter and future son-in-law chose to be married in her hometown church where Ken was the minister and had been since she was in the first grade. She wisely and gently informed Ken that she wanted him to be her dad and not the officiating minister. She and her fiancé chose a minister they knew from church camp where she had been a counselor and where he'd been a cook during the summer of their graduate school years. Ken was to have the pleasure of walking her down the aisle. And in our shared parenting, he and I were privileged to stand and give her away in marriage.

Ken and I hold a treasure of memories between us that are part of the matrix of our marriage. We have our fifty-one years of shared history documented in twenty-eight albums showcasing our engagement, wedding, and the birth and upbringing of our daughter. There are photos of graduations of our daughter and of me, anniversaries of Ken's ordination, and our living in England on two separate pulpit exchanges when our daughter was an infant and again as a three-year-old. We have records, videos, and photos of numerous dance recitals, birthday celebrations with each of us having had a surprise (a really big surprise) birthday party, summer holidays, and family gatherings. We have a marriage history packed with experiences that, as I look back, bring a smile. And as clear as the blue cloudless sky primarily dominates over the storms, the joyful times plainly overshadow the difficult ones. The rough times in some instances have provided opportunities where we grew individually in ways that led to life-altering patterns. I like to think that growth for one of us led to a more fulfilling marriage for us both.

We share a history of decisions, experiences, and compromises documented in our memories and my collection of journals. Ken and I have created this marriage and raised our daughter together. What we have created may be the strongest reason for why I stay.

About the Author

Donna Brazzi Barnes taught dental hygiene for over twenty years before earning a PhD in sociology from the University of California, San Francisco, after which she began a career teaching women's studies and continuing her research on women with HIV/AIDS in three US cities. Barnes has given talks at numerous national social science conferences, including the International AIDS Society Conference in Paris and International AIDS Conferences in Toronto and Barcelona. Her scholarship has been anthologized in *Women, Motherhood and Living with HIV/AIDS* (Springer, 2013), and two other books, as well as in various academic journals.

SELECTED TITLES FROM SHE WRITES PRESS

*She Writes Press is an independent publishing
company founded to serve women writers everywhere.
Visit us at www.shewritespress.com.*

*Flip-Flops After Fifty: And Other Thoughts on Aging I Remembered
to Write Down* by Cindy Eastman. $16.95, 978-1-938314-68-1. A
collection of frank and funny essays about turning fifty—and all the
emotional ups and downs that come with it.

*Her Name Is Kaur: Sikh American Women Write About Love,
Courage, and Faith* edited by Meeta Kaur. $17.95, 978-1-938314-
70-4. An eye-opening, multifaceted collection of essays by Sikh
American women exploring the concept of love in the context of
the modern landscape and influences that shape their lives.

*Mothering Through the Darkness: Women Open Up About the
Postpartum Experience* edited by Stephanie Sprenger and Jessica
Smock. $16.95, 978-1-63152-804-0. A collection of thirty powerful
essays aimed at spreading awareness and dispelling myths about
postpartum depression and perinatal mood disorders.

*Transforming Knowledge: Public Talks on Women's Studies, 1976-
2011* by Jean Fox O'Barr. $19.95, 978-1-938314-48-3. A collection
of essays addressing one woman's challenges faced and lessons
learned on the path to reframing—and effecting—feminist change.

Times They Were A-Changing: Women Remember the '60s & '70s
edited by Kate Farrell, Amber Lea Starfire, and Linda Joy Myers.
$16.95, 978-1-938314-04-9. Forty-eight powerful stories and
poems detailing the breakthrough moments experienced by women
during the '60s and '70s.

All the Ghosts Dance Free: A Memoir by Terry Cameron Baldwin.
$16.95, 978-1-63152-822-4. A poetic memoir that explores the
legacy of alcoholism and teen suicide in one woman's life—and her
efforts to create an authentic existence in the face of that legacy.